Behavior Therapy

A Series of Books in Psychology

Editors: **Richard C. Atkinson (1971–1975)**
Jonathan Freedman
Gardner Lindzey
Richard F. Thompson

Agras, Kazdin, and Wilson, *Behavior Therapy*
Aronson, *The Social Animal*
Aronson (ed.), *Readings About the Social Animal*
Bower, *Development in Infancy*
Bower, *A Primer of Infant Development*
Bower, *Human Development*
Cairns, *Social Development*
Cofer (ed.), *The Structure of Human Memory*
Edwards, *An Introduction to Linear Regression and Correlation*
Fantino and Logan, *The Experimental Analysis of Behavior*
Fantino and Reynolds, *Contemporary Psychology*
Freedman, *Crowding and Behavior*
Hassett, *A Primer of Psychophysiology*
Hintzman, *The Psychology of Learning and Memory*
Julien, *A Primer of Drug Action*
Kandel, *Cellular Basis of Behavior*
Kandel, *Behavioral Biology of Aplysia*
Klatzky, *Human Memory*
Kleinke, *Self-Perception*
Krantz, Atkinson, Luce, and Suppes (eds.), *Contemporary Developments in Mathematical Psychology: Learning, Memory, and Thinking*
Krantz, Atkinson, Luce, and Suppes (eds.), *Contemporary Developments in Mathematical Psychology: Measurement, Psychophysics, and Neural Information Processing*
Lee, *Experimental Design and Analysis*
Loehlin, Lindzey, and Spuhler, *Race Differences in Intelligence*
Lomax, Kagan, and Rosenkrantz, *Science and Patterns of Child Care*
Ludel, *Introduction to Sensory Processes*
Maser and Seligman (eds.), *Psychopathology: Experimental Models*
McClearn and DeFries, *Introduction to Behavioral Genetics*
Meyers and Grossen, *Behavioral Research*
Mussen and Eisenberg-Berg, *Roots of Caring, Sharing, and Helping*
Neisser, *Cognition and Reality*
Nordby and Hall, *A Guide to Psychologists and Their Concepts*
Norman and Rumelhart, *Explorations in Cognition*
Ornstein, *Psychology of Consciousness*
Ornstein (ed.), *The Nature of Human Consciousness*
Phillips, D. L., *Basic Statistics for Health Science Students*
Phillips, J. S., *Statistical Thinking*
Rachlin, *Behavior and Learning*
Rachman, *Fear and Courage*
Raphael, *The Thinking Computer*
Schank and Colby (eds.), *Computer Methods of Thought and Language*
Seligman, *Helplessness*
Teyler, *A Primer of Psychobiology*
Vasta, *Studying Children*
Vernon, *Intelligence*
Walters and Grusec, *Punishment*
Wickelgren, *How to Solve Problems*
Willemsen, *Understanding Statistical Reasoning*
Willemsen, *Understanding Infancy*
Willerman, *The Psychology of Individual and Group Differences*
Willerman and Turner (eds.), *Readings About Individual and Group Differences*

Behavior Therapy

Toward an Applied Clinical Science

W. Stewart Agras
Stanford University Medical School

Alan E. Kazdin
Pennsylvania State University

G. Terence Wilson
Rutgers University

W. H. Freeman and Company
San Francisco

Sponsoring Editor: W. Hayward Rogers; *Project Editor*: Betsy Dilernia; *Copyeditor*: Paul Monsour; *Designer*: Gary A. Head; *Production Coordinator*: Fran Mitchell; *Compositor*: Typesetting Services of California; *Printer and Binder*: Book Press.

Library of Congress Cataloging in Publication Data

Agras, W Stewart.
  Behavior therapy.

  (A Series of books in psychology)
  Bibliography: p.
  Includes index.
  1. Behavior therapy—Research. I. Kazdin, Alan E.,
joint author. II. Wilson, G. Terence, 1944–   joint
author. III. Title.
RC489.B4A36   616.8'914   78-32069
ISBN 0-7167-1086-2
ISBN 0-7167-1087-0 pbk.

Printed in the United States of America

1   2   3   4   5   6   7   8   9

Contents

Preface *vii*

1 *Behavior Therapy: Concepts and Characteristics* **1**

2 *The Efficacy of Behavior Therapy* **28**

3 *Conventional Clinical Outcome Research* **47**

4 *Alternative Strategies for Therapy Research* **67**

5 *Additional Therapy Research Strategies* **84**

6 *The Progression of Therapy Research* **105**

7 *Implications and Recommendations for Service Delivery, Training, and Research* **124**

8 *Summary and Overview* **148**

Index **169**

Preface

This volume is the outgrowth of a project initiated by Gardner Lindzey in his capacity as Director of the Center for Advanced Study in the Behavioral Sciences, with financial support derived largely from the Foundations Fund for Research in Psychiatry. Under these auspices, a group of behavioral scientists actively involved in the development of behavior therapy and modification were assembled at the Center for the 1976 – 1977 academic year. These fellows consisted of W. Stewart Agras, Nathan H. Azrin, Alan E. Kazdin, Walter Mischel, Stanley Rachman, and G. Terence Wilson. The seventh member of the group was Alexander L. George, a political scientist from Stanford University who was a fellow at the Center for a second time. (Interestingly, Alex's first fellowship year was 1956 – 1957, and one of the other Center fellows that year was Joseph Wolpe.) Specifically, what became known as the "behavioral group" was charged with preparing a report that evaluated the current status of outcome research bearing on behavior therapy, considered the methodological problems and solutions in this area of research, and made recommendations for future research directions.

The group met weekly throughout the year in discussions that covered a broad range of issues, only some of which were directly related to the immediate task of preparing the report. A special conference with a group of distinguished research psychiatrists —Peter Dews (Harvard University), Daniel X. Freedman (University of Chicago), Frederick C. Redlich (Yale University), Melvin Sabshin (American Psychiatric Association), and Robert S. Wallersteim (University of California Medical School, San Francisco— and Gardner Lindzey provided further direction and stimulus. The net result was the completion of a joint report (Agras et al., 1977) on the status of behavioral outcome research that was submitted to the Center in July 1977. Much of this report was based on a book on the evaluation of behavior therapy that Alan Kazdin and Terry Wilson (1978) completed during their stay at the Center.

As the report neared completion, a decision was taken to explore the possibility of preparing a less technical document that might be more appropriate for wider dissemination to other professionals and to funding and policy-making agencies. To this end a planning and writing committee was formed consisting of Stewart Agras, Alan Kazdin, and Terry Wilson. A draft version of the present volume was put together and circulated to the other members of the group following their return to their home institutions. Armed with this feedback, the three of us reassembled at the Center in March 1978 to make final revisions. The product that emerged goes beyond the boundaries of behavior therapy and is addressed to the more general issues of future directions for research on the development, application, and evaluation of psychological treatment methods. Inevitably, in this process the present volume came to reflect the particular interests and conceptual commitments of its three authors—Agras, Kazdin, and Wilson. It must be emphasized that this volume would never have been conceived let alone completed without the invaluable assistance, support, and substantive contributions of all group members. Some of the content is drawn directly from the group's final report to the Center (Agras et al., 1977), and much of the thinking expressed herein derives from our group meetings and numerous joint and separate discussions of these and related issues. We wish to express our appreciation to our fellow group members—good friends and respected colleagues one and all. Nonetheless, we must assume full and final responsibility for the views expressed here. The responsibility is shared equally among us; the order of authorship is alphabetical.

The opportunity to complete this book was made possible by our fellowships at the Center for Advanced Study in the Behavioral Sciences. W. Stewart Agras received financial support from the National Institute of Mental Health (1 T 32 — MH14581) and the Foundations Fund for Research in Psychiatry; Nathan H. Azrin from the Spender Foundation, the National Institute for Mental Health (1 T 32 — MH14581), and the Foundations Fund for Research in Psychiatry; Alexander L. George from the Foundations Fund for Research in Psychiatry, the National Science Foundation (Stanford grant), and Stanford University; Alan E. Kazdin from the Foundations Fund for Research in Psychiatry, the Spencer Foundation, the National Institute of Mental Health (1 T 32 — MH14581), and Pennsylvania State University; Walter Mischel from the Foundations Fund for Research in Psychiatry, the National Institute for Mental Health (MH-06830); Stanley Rachman from the Foundations Fund for Research in Psychiatry; and G. Terence Wilson from the Foundations Fund for Research in Psychiatry, the National Institute of Mental Health (1 T 32 —MH14581), and Rutgers—The State University of New Jersey.

Finally, it is with special pleasure that we express our gratitude to the Center, its staff, and its Director, Gardner Lindzey. Their kindness and congeniality are fundamental to making this lovely place the idyllic social and intellectual haven it has proven to be. Other friends deserving special mention are Margaret Amara and Christine Hoth, who provided us with incomparable library services and daily cheer, and Kay Jenks, who helped type earlier versions of this manuscript, smoothed all our arrangements, and provided invaluable moral support throughout.

January 1979   W. Stewart Agras
                               Alan E. Kazdin
                               G. Terence Wilson

                               Center for Advanced Study
                               in the Behavioral Sciences,
                               Stanford, California

Behavior Therapy

1

Behavior Therapy: Concepts and Characteristics

Behavior therapy is a relatively new approach to the assessment and treatment of clinical disorders.[1] It was only two decades ago that Wolpe (1958) completed his landmark text on a psychological approach to the treatment of clinical disorders, which has since come to be called behavior therapy. Although still controversial in some quarters, the doctrinaire attitudes and professional hostility that behavior therapy once faced have largely given way to acceptance. Behavior therapy has had a profound effect on psychology and education. It is well represented in doctoral training programs in clinical psychology in this country, some of the most respected programs being primarily if not exclusively behavioral in orientation. A lesser but nonetheless noticeable impact on psychiatry and social work is also evident. In 1973 a special task force of the American Psychiatric Association resolved that behavior therapy has

---

[1]The term *behavior therapy* is used synonymously with *behavior modification* throughout this volume. Although some writers have distinguished between these terms, usage has not been consistent and little has been achieved in the process.

"much to offer informed clinicians in the service of modern clinical and social psychiatry." Practitioners of behavior therapy are everywhere in demand, and psychiatrists, psychologists, and social workers have adopted many of its methods. In addition to advances in the United States, Canada, western Europe, Australia, and New Zealand, active centers of behavioral research and therapy are found in Latin American countries, such as Brazil and Mexico. Behavior therapy accounts for a significant part of the psychological and psychiatric literature. According to the *Psychological Abstracts Annual Index*, a widely accepted source of publication activity in psychology, the number of publications on behavior therapy had surpassed that for psychoanalysis by 1972. Numerous scientific journals are devoted exclusively to behavior therapy. The literature is so large and diverse that an *Annual Review* series on the theory and practice of behavior therapy was begun in 1973 (Franks and Wilson, 1973 — 1978), and a specialized journal of abstracts of the contemporary literature recently established. And there are no signs of any slowing of this literature explosion.

Of singular importance is the fact that the nature and scope of behavior therapy are showing relatively rapid change. Clinical practice reflects the development of new techniques and the modification of existing methods; the range of procedures and problems that are being researched shows exponential growth, and theoretical views, often sharply conflicting, are the subject of lively debate. To obtain perspective on the development of behavior therapy and to understand current trends, it is necessary to review briefly the major themes in the emergence of behavior therapy as a therapeutic alternative to more traditional psychotherapeutic approaches (see Kazdin, 1978, for a detailed discussion of the history of behavior therapy). In attempting to distill the essence of contemporary behavior therapy from the developments of the past 20 years, we are not unmindful of Boring's (1950) injunction in *A History of Experimental Psychology*—that he spoke "with confidence" of developments occurring up to 20 years before his book, with "less assurance of the next decade," and with "gratuitous courage" for the most recent decade! Nonetheless, identifying some of the major accomplishments and trends that have emerged in this burgeoning field does seem possible. This volume is designed to give a brief overview of the field. In this chapter the different emphases and theoretical positions within behavior therapy are briefly reviewed and the characteristics that presently define the field described. The following chapter samples some of the evidence on the applicability and outcome efficacy of behavior therapy. Chapter 3 highlights the conceptual and methodological inadequacies of much of conventional therapy outcome research. Chapters 4, 5, and 6 provide different methodological prescriptions for innovative and improved research on treatment evaluation, together with an analysis of the interrelationships among different methodological strategies and the overall progression of treatment outcome research. The implications of this developing science of psychological treatment for service delivery, training, and research policy are discussed in Chapter 7. Chapter 8 summarizes the major issues, conclusions, and recommendations that are presented throughout this volume.

A Brief History

Despite numerous historical influences and antecedents, the origins of contemporary behavior therapy can be traced directly to separate but related developments in the 1950s. A major impetus was the growth of operant conditioning in the United States and the extension of these principles and procedures to personal and social problems. This development was spurred by Skinner's (1953) book *Science and Human Behavior,* in which he criticized the prevailing psychodynamic approach and reconceptualized psychotherapy in behavioral terms. Psychotherapy was recast as an educational rather than a medical endeavor, and behavior was recognized as important in its own right instead of being indicative of a more basic underlying problem.

In 1959, Eysenck, working at the Institute of Psychiatry in London, defined behavior therapy as the application of "modern learning theory" to the treatment of psychiatric disorders. The phrase "modern learning theory" referred to the behavioristic formulations of learning theorists such as Pavlov, Hull, Mowrer, and to a much lesser extent, Skinner. Eysenck conceptualized *behavior* therapy as a more scientifically acceptable and more therapeutically effective alternative to *psychotherapy,* which was criticized as unscientific and lacking in proof of its efficacy. Finally Wolpe (1958), in his text *Psychotherapy by Reciprocal Inhibition,* introduced several important treatment techniques based on neo-Hullian conditioning principles and his own research on the elimination of experimentally induced neurotic reactions in cats.

These early developments in behavior therapy represented an accommodation of interests rather than an identity of views. The psychoanalytic establishment was the common foe; the quasi-disease model of the etiology and treatment of clinical disorders was uniformly rejected; and the lack of evidence supporting the efficacy of traditional psychotherapeutic methods was emphasized. Despite their differences, however, the early behavioral approaches (neo-Hullian and operant) did share some fundamental assumptions aside from the natural bond that derives from concerted opposition to a common opponent. They both sought to ground their principles and procedures in scientifically established learning principles. Both expressed a commitment to experimental method and stressed the importance of critically evaluating the therapeutic outcome of their methods. Importantly, and in contrast to previous approaches, they both rejected the psychoanalytic model and proposed explicitly formulated alternative views of the development, maintenance, and modification of clinical disorders.

Behavior therapy is not a monolithic structure. During the 1960s the differences among behavioral approaches became more apparent as they were increasingly accepted and as the field became more self-critical. Unlike Eysenck and Wolpe, who defined behavior therapy primarily in terms of the application of conditioning principles to clinical disorders, Ullmann and Krasner (1969) offered a more encompassing definition of behavior therapy as "treatment deducible from the sociopsychological model that aims to alter a person's behavior *directly* through the application of general psychological principles." As such, behavior therapy was contrasted with traditional treatment that was "deducible from a medical or psychoanalytic model that aims to alter a person's behavior *indirectly* by first altering intrapsychic organizations." In this conception, the defining characteristic was the *model* of abnormal behavior rather than the specific principles or procedures that constituted therapeutic intervention.

Lazarus (1971, 1976), who studied under Wolpe, later developed what he termed *broad-spectrum be-*

havior therapy, emphasizing the need for a multifaceted clinical approach that went beyond the limits of early behavior therapy. The resulting controversy created a rift between the proponents of this approach and proponents of Wolpe's. Lastly, Bandura (1969) detailed the most comprehensive and sophisticated analysis of behavior therapy to date within the framework of social learning theory. In contrast to previous approaches, Bandura's influential book emphasized the importance of vicarious learning, cognitive mediating processes, and self-regulatory function in human behavior.

Now, in the 1970s, behavior therapy is more mature and considerably more complex and varied than in any of its earlier stages. Gone is the unbridled enthusiasm of the late 1950s and early 1960s, replaced by a more cautious optimism. Outdated are simplistic definitions of behavior therapy as the application of learning theory to clinical disorders. As Kazdin and Wilson (1978, p. 1) put it:

Contemporary behavior therapy is marked by a diversity of views, a broad range of heterogeneous procedures with different theoretical rationales, and open debate about conceptual bases, methodological requirements, and evidence of efficacy. In short, there is no clearly agreed upon or commonly accepted definition of behavior therapy.

Broadly conceived of, the different approaches in contemporary behavior therapy include applied behavior analysis, a neobehavioristic mediational model, social learning theory, and cognitive behavior modification.[2] The purpose in delineating these different approaches is to identify the scope of the field.

---

[2]Not addressed here is Lazarus's (1976) multimodal behavior theory, which is often identified as one of the various treatment approaches within behavior therapy. Despite a major overlap in the therapeutic techniques that are employed, multimodal therapy can be differentiated from

This classification schema for referring to the different approaches is arbitrary and by no means the only way in which the subject can be organized.

Current Conceptualizations

Applied Behavior Analysis

Applied behavior analysis can be defined as the application of behavioral methods to modify behaviors of personal and social importance (Baer, Wolf, and Risley, 1968). There are several distinctive features of applied behavior analysis. First, the emphasis is exclusively on overt behaviors in applied settings. Exemplified by the research in the *Journal of Applied Behavior Analysis*, this approach is philosophically consistent with Skinner's doctrine of radical behaviorism. Applied behavior analysis relies on techniques derived from operant conditioning, the fundamental assumption of which is that behavior is a function of its consequences. As Skinner (1971, p. 211) declared: "A person does not act upon the world, the world acts upon him." Accordingly, treatment procedures are based on altering the functional relationships between overt behaviors and their consequences. Cognitive process and private events are not regarded as the proper subjects of scientific analysis; rather, they are viewed as irrelevant or epiphenomenal.

A second characteristic of applied behavior analysis is its methodology for evaluating treatment effects. The focus is on the intensive study of the individual subject, similar to the approach of the exper-

---

behavior therapy as it is discussed here on both conceptual and methodological grounds. Lazarus himself has recently distinguished multimodal from behavior therapy.

imental analysis of behavior in animal laboratory research. The development of a number of different
single-case experimental designs in which the subject serves as his or her own control represents a
signal contribution of the applied operant approach.
This innovative methodological contribution is discussed in greater detail in Chapter 4.

A third characteristic of applied behavior analysis is the focus on powerful environmental variables
that produce significant changes in behavior. This
search for potent variables reflects the emphasis on
producing clinically important changes that are
sufficiently obvious to preclude the need for statistical analysis.

A fourth characteristic of applied behavior analysis is the use of a wide range of techniques based on
reinforcement, punishment, extinction, stimulus control, and other learning principles that have been derived from laboratory research. These techniques have
been applied on an individual basis or to entire groups
of individuals as, for example, in the token economy.
These operant techniques were originally extended to
populations considered to have limited cognitive ca-
pacities, such as institutionalized chronic psychotic
patients and the severely mentally retarded. However,
the range of treatment applications transcends any
simple population with common characteristics.
Applied behavior analysis includes interventions in
institutional, rehabilitation, and educational settings
as well as the community at large, the home, and
outpatient treatment.

The Neobehavioristic Mediational
S-R Model

This approach has been defined as the application of
the principles of conditioning, especially classical

conditioning and counterconditioning, to the etiology and treatment of abnormal behavior. It derives from the pioneering contributions of Eysenck, Rachman, and Wolpe, who attempted to ground the theory and practice of behavior therapy in the learning theories of Pavlov, Guthrie, Hull, Mowrer, and Miller. Unlike the operant approach, the S-R model has always been mediational, with intervening variables and hypothetical constructs prominently featured. Exemplifying the mediational nature of this approach is the central importance assigned to the construct of anxiety. In two-factor theory, a major part of the theoretical foundations of this approach, an underlying anxiety drive is assumed to motivate overt avoidance behavior. The treatment techniques of systematic desensitization and flooding, which are most closely associated with this model, are both directed toward the extinction of the underlying anxiety that is assumed to maintain phobic disorders. This model of avoidance behavior is explicitly rejected by operant conditioners. Private events, especially imagery, have been an integral part of several techniques identified with this approach, including systematic desensitization and covert conditioning techniques such as covert sensitization. The rationale behind all these methods is that covert processes follow the laws of learning that govern overt behaviors.

The neobehavioristic nature of this approach dictates that private events such as imagining an anxiety-eliciting occurrence are anchored to antecedent and consequent operational referents. Thus, psychophysiological studies have shown that symbolic representation of a feared stimulus produces autonomic arousal similar to that evoked by the stimulus itself. Moreover, these arousal responses have been shown to covary systematically with the introduction and repeated presentation of hierarchy items during systematic desensitization in a manner consistent with conditioning concepts.

Although symbolic processes such as imagery are fundamental features of the behavioral techniques associated with this approach, cognitive activities in this view of behavior therapy have always been defined in terms of stimulus and response. Cognitive formulations of these mediational constructs have been rejected by proponents of this approach. Wolpe (1976), for example, relegated the significance of cognitive interventions in therapy to the provision of background material and the correction of clients' misconceptions. This emphasis on conditioning as opposed to cognitions as the conceptual basis of behavior therapy is not surprising in view of the early reliance on principles from the animal conditioning laboratory and the behavioristic reaction against the mentalistic concepts and methods of psychotherapy.

The S-R conditioning theory on which several behavioral procedures have been based has been the target of increasing criticism. Eysenck (1976) recently conceded that traditional conditioning theory is untenable as a comprehensive explanation of fear reduction techniques. Similarly, Rachman (1977) confirmed previous objections in indicating how conditioning theory provides an inadequate basis for explaining the acquisition of fear. Eysenck has proposed a new conditioning model of the development of phobic disorders that better accommodates recent research and clinical findings.

Social Learning Theory

The social learning approach to behavior therapy is a comprehensive analysis of human functioning in which behavior is assumed to be developed and maintained on the basis of three separate but interacting regulatory systems (Bandura, 1977b). Some response patterns are regulated primarily by external stimulus events and are affected largely by paired experiences. The influence of external reinforcement constitutes a second form of influence, while the third and most important system of regulatory influence operates through cognitive mediational processes.

In terms of a social learning analysis, the influence of environmental events on the acquisition and regulation of behavior is largely determined by cognitive processes. These cognitive factors govern what environmental influences are attended to, how they are perceived, and whether they might affect future action. In this analysis, classical conditioning does not occur automatically simply on the basis of the temporal contiguity of two stimuli. Conditioned reactions are interpreted as self-activated, learned expectations. Similarly, reinforcement is not viewed as an automatic strengthener of behavior but as a source of information and incentive that regulates behavior. The technique of modeling, or vicarious learning, exemplifies some of the key aspects of social learning theory. In modeling, learning is assumed to occur through coding of representational processes based on exposure to instructional, observational, or imagined material. Learning occurs through observation alone. No response need be emitted nor any reinforcement administered by the therapist.

Social learning theory is based on a reciprocal determinism model of causal processes in human behavior. Psychological functioning involves a reciprocal interaction among three interlocking sets of influences: behavior, cognitive processes, and environmental factors. Bandura (1977a, p. 345) put it as follows:

Personal and environmental factors do not function as independent determinants; rather they determine each other. Nor can 'persons' be considered causes independent of their behavior. It is largely through their actions that people produce the environmental conditions that affect their behavior in a reciprocal fashion. The experiences generated by behavior also partly determine what individuals think, expect, and can do, which in turn, affect their subsequent behavior.

In this conceptual scheme, a person is neither driven by internal forces nor is a passive reactor to external events. Rather, a person is both the agent as well as the object of environmental influence.

Another characteristic of social learning theory is related to the notion that the person is an agent of change: The theory emphasizes the human capacity for self-directed behavioral change. The operant conditioning view of behavioral self-control is really an analysis of external situational control that fundamentally denies the notion of self-control. In addition to the acquisition and maintenance of behavior, activation and persistence of behavior is assumed to be determined largely by cognitive mechanisms. Cognitive processes are used to explain how learning experiences have lasting effects and serve to activate future actions.

The social learning view of behavior therapy is a theoretical integration of the different sources of influence that determine behavior. This is illustrated in Bandura's conceptual analysis of the modification of phobic behavior. The key assumption in this analysis is that psychological treatment methods produce changes in a person's expectations of self-efficacy. Self-efficacy expectations are modified by different sources of psychological changes (e.g., systematic desensitization) and verbal persuasion (e.g., traditional psychotherapy).

Cognitive Behavior Modification

The most recent development within behavior therapy is the emergence of what is referred to as cognitive behavior modification, or cognitive behavior therapy (Mahoney, 1974). This approach encompasses a number of diverse procedures, some of which have developed outside the mainstream of behavior therapy. The techniques most characteristic of cognitive behavior modification are referred to as cognitive restructuring. These methods are predicated on the assumption that clinical disorders are the result of maladaptive or faulty thought patterns. The task of therapy is to identify faulty thought patterns and replace them with more adaptive cognitions.

The most prominent method of cognitive restructuring is Ellis's (1970) rational-emotive therapy. According to this approach, emotional disorders are the consequence of specific irrational assumptions or self-statements. An example of the cognitions that Ellis asserts are irrational is: "It is a dire necessity for an adult to be loved by everyone for everything he does." People do not necessarily tell themselves these irrational statements in everyday situations; they are assumed to be automatic, over-learned responses. Ellis's approach and all other cognitive restructuring methods rest on the assumption that it is not experience per se but the person's perception of that experience that produces neurotic disorders. The neurotic distorts objective reality. Treatment consists of verbal persuasion and logical argument directed towards altering the client's irrational ideas. Although not always emphasized, specific behavioral tasks are also used to modify faulty perceptions of important life events.

A second variation of cognitive restructuring is Meichenbaum's (1977) self-instructional training. The rationale for this approach derives, first, from Ellis's rational-emotive therapy and its focus on faulty interpretations of experience and, second, from the normal developmental sequence in which children acquire internal speech and verbal-symbolic control over their behavior. After identifying maladaptive thoughts (self-statements), the therapist models appropriate behavior while verbalizing constructive, problem-solving self-instructions. The client then engages in the behavior while verbalizing aloud the self-instructions modeled by the therapist and then while rehearsing them cognitively.

A third variation of cognitive restructuring is Beck's (1976) cognitive therapy. As with rational-emotive therapy and self-instructional training, the goal of cognitive therapy is the replacement of faulty thought patterns with more adaptive cognitions. In addition to verbal-cognitive means, Beck emphasizes the importance of behavioral methods in altering faulty thought patterns. In short, behavioral procedures are used to change cognitive processes. The behavorial methods used include specific activity schedules, graded tasks aimed at providing successful coping experiences, and other homework assignments tailored to the individual client's case. Cognitive techniques used by Beck include procedures designed to facilitate a more objective and detached view of emotion-arousing events.

There are a number of other procedures that

have been included in cognitive behavior modification, including problem solving, stress inoculation, coping skills training, thought stopping, attribution therapy, and others. In many cases, these techniques represent procedures not addressed by other conceptualizations and approaches within behavior therapy; in other cases, the procedures merely emphasize components of a given technique whose interpretation has yet to be resolved.

The Behavior Therapies: The Common Core

Although the preceding approaches often involve conceptual differences, behavior therapists maintain a common core of fundamental assumptions. In the ultimate analysis, behavior therapy is defined in terms of two basic characteristics: (1) a psychological model of human behavior that differs fundamentally from the traditional intrapsychic, psychodynamic, or quasi-disease model of mental illness; and (2) a commitment to scientific method, measurement, and evaluation. Each of these characteristics has implications for assessment, modification, and evaluation.

The emphasis on the psychological as opposed to quasi-disease model of abnormal behavior has the following therapeutic consequences:

• Abnormal behavior that is not a function of specific brain dysfunction or biochemical disturbance is assumed to be governed by the same principles that regulate normal behavior.

• Many types of abnormal behavior formerly regarded as illnesses in themselves or as signs and symptoms of illness are better construed as non-pathological "problems of living" (key examples include neurotic reactions, various forms of sexual deviance, and conduct disorders).

• Most abnormal behavior is assumed to be acquired and maintained in the same manner as normal behavior; it can be treated through the application of behavioral procedures.

• Behavioral assessment focuses on the *current* determinants of behavior rather than the post hoc analysis of possible historical antecedents.

Specificity is the hallmark of behavioral assessment and treatment, and it is assumed that the person is best understood and described by what he or she does in a particular situation.

• Treatment requires a fine-grain analysis of the problem into components or subparts and is targeted at these components specifically and systematically.

• Treatment strategies are individually tailored to different problems in different individuals.

• Understanding the development of a psychological problem is not essential for producing behavior change. Conversely, success in changing a problem behavior does not imply knowledge about its etiology.

• Since behavior change occurs in a specific social context, therapeutic interventions may result in side effects, i.e., changes in behaviors that were not the focus of treatment. These are not necessarily deleterious effects or a product of "symptom substitution." More often than not these broader treatment effects are positive outcomes.

• Behavior therapy involves a commitment to an applied science approach. This includes the following characteristics:

An explicit, testable conceptual framework.

Treatment that is either derived from or at least consistent with the content and method of experimental-clinical psychology.

Therapeutic techniques that can be described with sufficient precision to be measured objectively and be replicated.

The experimental evaluation of treatment methods and concepts.

The emphasis on innovative research strategies that allow rigorous evaluation of specific methods applied to particular problems instead of global assessment of ill-defined procedures applied to heterogeneous problems.

Current Research and Practice

Research Activities

Given the commitment of behavior therapy to scientific method and evaluation, it is not surprising that the outstanding finding that emerges from any investigation of current research is the impressive amount of such activity. Research runs the gamut from investigations of fundamental mechanisms of psychological functioning and change to the evaluation of multifaceted treatment outcome strategies. Controlled studies of the development and assessment of specific behavior change methods applied to particular problems have been especially frequent. To take one example, a recent review of the experimental evidence on systematic desensitization noted that over 70 studies had been published between 1970 and 1974, and this figure came from sampling only five of the many journals that publish studies on behavior therapy (Kazdin and Wilcoxon, 1976). Although systematic desensitization is one of the more intensively researched behavioral techniques, numerous other behavioral treatment methods have been the subject of systematic and searching experimental analyses. We can safely conclude that never before have psychological treatment procedures been subjected to so much experimental scrutiny.

A major contribution of behavior therapy has been the development of innovative research strategies for the study of treatment development and outcome. These methodological strategies range from single-case experimental designs to a variety of different group designs, including highly controlled laboratory-based studies, more applied evaluations of complex treatment packages, and comparative outcome evaluations. As we will see, these different methodological strategies go well beyond conventional research methods and permit more refined empirical analyses of specific treatment questions. Nor are they confined to the evaluation of behavioral methods—they can be applied to all psychological treatment methods. Related to this expansion of research method are significant advances in the measurement of treatment outcome. The development of multiple subjective and objective measures of therapeutic outcome, which have been extensively assessed in terms of reliability, validity, and utility, has opened new frontiers of outcome research.

Inevitably, the quality of this greatly increased volume of therapy research has not always been commensurate with the exacting ideals of an impartial scientific approach. Many studies have been trivial or of dubious relevance to therapeutic outcome. Other studies have suffered from one or more of a variety of common methodological shortcomings. Long-term evaluations of treatment outcomes have been conspicuous by their relative absence. All in all, however, significant progress has been made, and several major research accomplishments registered (Franks and Wilson, 1973 – 1978; Kazdin and Wilson, 1978). A summary review of the present status of behavioral research and of prescriptions for new directions and future research policy is presented in the following chapters of this volume.

Clinical Practice

Behavior therapy encompasses a broad spectrum of different treatment techniques, including the following: methods for reducing anxiety or avoidance behavior, such as relaxation training, systematic desensitization, flooding, and participant modeling; a variety of self-control procedures for regulating diverse disorders, such as the addictive behaviors; modeling and reinforcement techniques for developing social skills and enhanced behavioral repertoires; and other specific methods for eliminating unwanted or undesirable responses.

Whereas research has often focused on specific treatment techniques applied to individual, well-defined target problems, the clinical practice of behavior therapy usually involves complex and multifaceted treatment programs. The therapist flexibly draws on the psychological principles and procedures outlined above in tailoring treatment to the individual client's particular needs. Relatively straightforward problems might require no more than a few weeks for effective treatment, but more complex disorders will often involve extensive therapeutic contact that might take months or even longer.

Behavioral assessment of clinical problems typically departs from traditional psychodiagnostic procedures on both conceptual and procedural grounds. The emphasis is on identifying the specific variables that are currently maintaining the problem. Past experiences in the client's life are addressed only to the extent that they actively contribute to the current problem. A complete behavioral assessment reveals all the current causes that determine the client's presenting problem. Consider, for example, the assessment of a client with alcoholism. The straw-man behavior therapist would be expected to attempt to modify the excessive drinking behavior directly, possible using electrical aversion conditioning, without further probing. However, an analysis of the circumstances under which the drinking occurs might show that the client abuses alcohol when he or she is depressed. The conditions that result in depression must then be determined. Depression may result from marital disharmony. If so, the client's marital problems and depressive reactions are viewed as important antecedents of drinking. Behavioral treatment of this client's presenting problem, i.e., alcoholism, would be incomplete and probably ineffective if therapy did not include the marital relationship and ensuing depression.

Behavior therapists have rarely resorted to standardized psychlogical tests in carrying out an assessment. The level of specificity required by a behavioral assessment and the fact that it is intervention oriented necessitates alternative assessment methods. The interview is a major source of information, differing from more traditional therapies in the degree of specificity with which the analysis of current maintaining variables is pursued. This assessment is aided by asking the client to keep detailed daily records of the target problem. Other commonly used assessment procedures include the use of imagery, e.g., asking clients to imagine a particular situation and then report what they feel, think, and do in that context; role playing, e.g., rehearsing an interpersonal interaction instead of merely describing it; direct behavioral observation, e.g., requesting that a mother record the frequency and nature of her child's problem behavior; and psychophysiological measurement, e.g., monitoring sexual arousal through the direct measurement of penile tumescence or vaginal blood flow (cf. Ciminero, Calhoun, and Adams, 1977).

In addition to individual treatment, behavior therapy is often conducted in groups. Interventions at the broader social level, especially in institutions and the community, are also common. Fundamental to behavior modification in these broader social influence settings is the use of nonprofessionals such as parents, teachers, psychiatric aides, and peer groups as mediators of behavior change programs. The therapist acts as a consultant directing these psychological assistants, who have direct contact with the target person or population in the effective use of behavioral procedures (cf. Nietzel et al., 1977).

Common Questions
About Behavior Therapy

A comprehensive evaluation of the criticisms directed
at behavior therapy and the numerous theoretical
debates among its proponents is beyond the scope of
this volume. A few key conceptual issues are discussed here briefly, however, because of their intrin-
sic importance and because of the need to clarify
some misconceptions.

Is Behavior Therapy Behavioristic?

It is important to distinguish between philosophical
or radical behaviorism and methodological behaviorism. Philosophical behaviorism holds that conscious
experience is fictional or epiphenomenal and posits
exclusive environmental determinism of all behavior.
Philosophical behaviorism was the now-discredited
doctrine of J. B. Watson, who, in the second decade
of this century, attempted to reduce all experience to
basic glandular secretions and muscular movements.
Skinner has labeled himself a radical behaviorist in
that he denies the existence of nonphysical processes in human behavior and asserts that behavior
is totally controlled by environmental variables. Consistent with this view, applied behavior analysts have
largely ignored cognitive processes, which are assumed to be a direct function of environmental variables.

Methodological behaviorism is a commitment to
scientific method that emphasizes an empirical-
functional approach rather than the content matter
under investigation. With the exception of those indi-

viduals who work within a strict operant conditioning framework, the behaviorism of contemporary behavior therapists is methodological rather than radical. According to most behavior therapists, the scientific study of internal or mediational processes is both necessary and desirable provided that they are anchored firmly to observable antecedent and consequent events. This emphasis is especially evident in the social learning theory and cognitive behavior modification approaches, fundamental tenets of which are that cognitions exert causal influence on behavior.

Is Behavior Therapy a Superficial Form of Treatment?

One of the earliest objections to behavior therapy was that it was a superficial treatment that would result in "symptom substitution." Contrary to earlier conceptual confusion, more recent theoretical analyses have shown that behavior therapy is not a symptomatic form of treatment that ignores the causes of behavior (Bandura, 1969). Both behavioral and psychodynamic treatments attempt to modify the "underlying causes" of behavior; the difference is what the proponents of each approach regard as causes. Psychodynamic formulations favor hypothetical unconscious determinants of behavior; behavior modification, in contrast, considers the causes to be antecedent, mediational, and consequent variables that are controlling or maintaining the inappropriate response patterns.

Symptom substitution has been a confused and confusing notion. The conceptual problems of symptom substitution do not extend to the more empiri-

cally based phenomenon that changes in target behavior may be associated with changes in nontarget
behavior. These correlated changes are usually positive, and in the rare instances when changes have
been adverse, they can be explained more par-
simoniously as correlated changes than as substitute
symptoms. Specific target behaviors are frequently
members of broader response classes. Some data
suggest that altering a specific behavior may produce
changes within the entire response class. Behavior
change does not take place in a social vacuum. Behavior changes will influence the social environment
in which the individual functions. Changes in the
environment in turn are likely to alter further responses of the individual beyond those specifically
addressed in treatment.

*Is Behavior Therapy a Mechanistic
or Impersonal Approach?*

Behavior therapy, no less than any other form of
psychotherapy, is a personally and professionally
challenging endeavor that requires considerable
therapist skill, sensitivity, and clinical acumen for effective application. Direct study of behavior therapists and reports of their clients tend to support
this conclusion. Perhaps most important, the docu-
mented efficacy of behavior therapy attests to the
fact that behavior therapists generally possess these
skills. Although it has not always been emphasized,
and while the scientific language in which behavior
therapy is typically described often obscures it, the
therapeutic relationship is of significance in clinical
behavior therapy (Wilson and Evans, 1978).

In earlier behavioral formulations, relationship
factors, including loosely defined concepts of

placebo, therapeutic expectations, mutual trust, and empathy, were relegated to the secondary status of nonspecific variables. These were relatively ignored and held in sharp contrast to specific behavioral techniques derived from learning priniciples. In more recent conceptualizations of behavior therapy within a broader social learning framework, it is argued that the interpersonal factors that characterize the therapeutic relationship are an integral part of behavior therapy. It is more accurate, therefore, to note that although many so-called nonspecific variables remain to be specified, they are neither intrinsically unspecifiable nor qualitatively very different from other variables in planned behavior change. By recognizing the therapist's interpersonal behavior as a part of the social influence process that is therapy, behavior therapy can be viewed as a more human practice than some critics have acknowledged. Moreover, relationship variables can be enhanced and deliberately tailored to achieve specific treatment goals.

What Is the Role of Ethics in Behavior Therapy?

Behavior therapy has on occasion been depicted as a manipulative or Machiavellian approach that unilaterally imposes treatment goals on clients. Detailed discussions of ethical considerations in behavior therapy are presented elsewhere (Azrin et al., 1977; Davison and Stuart, 1975; Goldiamond, 1974; Stolz et al., 1977). Suffice it here to summarize some of the basic issues.

One of the issues is *who* determines the goals of therapy. Because it is fundamental to behavior therapy that the client should have the major say in setting treatment goals, it is important that the fully informed client consents to and participates in this activity. A distinction is drawn between how behavior is to be changed—an empirical question in which the therapist is presumably expert—and what the objectives are. The latter is a matter of value judgments that the client must ultimately determine.

To believe that the therapist plays no role in influencing the selection of therapy goals would be naive. The major contribution of the therapist in this regard is to assist clients in the fundamental decision-making process by helping them to generate alternative courses of action and to analyze the consequences of pursuing various goals. Since this process inevitably involves an expression of the therapist's own values, it is incumbent on the therapist to identify his or her values and, to the extent that they are relevant to the therapeutic interaction, to suggest how they might affect the therapist's analysis of therapeutic goals.

Selecting goals is far more complicated in the case of institutionalized clients or clients who are too disturbed (e.g., many psychotics) to participate meaningfully in the determination of treatment objectives. In the latter case it becomes necessary to waive the fundamental ethical requirement that governs the therapist's behavior—the client's informed consent which by definition calls for a voluntary, competent, and knowledgeable choice. To ensure that treatment is in the client's best interests, it is important to monitor program goals and procedures through some form of professional and institutional review.

Of course, the ethical imperative of informed consent, professional accountability, and quality control of treatment are common to *all* forms of psychological and psychiatric treatment. Little is unique about behavior therapy in this respect. Although behavior therapy has often been singled out for scrutiny, all forms of therapy involve social influence. The issue is not whether clients' behavior should be influenced; it inevitably is. The critical ethical question is whether therapists are aware of this influence. Behavior therapy entails an explicit recognition of this influence process and emphasizes specific, client-oriented behavioral objectives. This can be contrasted with some traditional therapies, in which treatment goals are not always clearly specified and hence are more easily influenced, albeit unwittingly, by the therapists' values and theoretical allegiance. Behavior therapists have been in the forefront of attempts to formulate procedures that guarantee the human rights and personal dignity of clients, including homosexuals, the retarded, mental hospital patients, and school children, among others.

2

The Efficacy of Behavior Therapy

A review of the evidence for the efficacy of behavior therapy would require an analysis of the results of all behavioral techniques that have been applied to an exceptionally wide range of psychological, medical, and educational problems. Such a review of the burgeoning literature is beyond the scope of this or any other single volume. In this chapter, therefore, we will provide a few illustrations of the scope of behavior therapy and of the evidence supporting its effectiveness. Further considerations of its effectiveness will be found in Chapter 6. Two sources of evidence can be examined to evaluate the efficacy of behavior therapy. The first consists of the outcome evidence with specific psychiatric, psychological, and behavioral disorders. In these studies, a behavioral method is compared with another behavioral method, with a placebo control group; or with no treatment at all. The second consists of comparing the relative efficacy of behavior therapy and an alternative therapeutic technique derived from a different conceptual basis. Such comparative outcome research is reviewed in Chapter 3.

Clinical Problem Areas

The outcome evidence encompasses the full gamut of psychiatric and psychological disorders. For present purposes, evidence is selected from the treatment of neurotic disorders, sexual dysfunction and deviance, marital discord, addictive behaviors, psychotic disorders, childhood disorders, mental retardation, and other disorders.

Neurotic Disorders

The pioneers of the clinical practice of behavior therapy with adults, such as Wolpe (1958) and Lazarus (1958, 1961), treated predominantly neurotic outpatients. As a result, behavior therapy is often identified as being almost exclusively concerned with the treatment of neurotic disorders. Indeed, many of the best known and most widely used behavioral techniques were developed within the context of treating anxiety reactions and avoidance behavior. These include systematic desensitization, relaxation training, reinforced practice, flooding, modeling and its variants, response prevention, and assertiveness training.

Attention has been focused on anxiety and the phobic reactions. Of the multitude of methods used to treat anxiety-related disorders, systematic desensitization must rank as the most intensively researched therapy on record. For present purposes, reference need only be made to the conclusions of exhaustive and methodologically searching reviews of the desensitization research literature. For example, Paul (1969, p. 159) concluded as follows:

The findings were overwhelmingly positive, and for the first time in the history of psychological treatments, a specific treatment package reliably produced measurable benefits for clients across a broad range of distressing problems in which anxiety was of fundamental importance.

Leitenberg (1976, p. 131) concluded that "systematic desensitization is demonstrably more effective than both no treatment and every psychotherapy variant with which it has so far been compared." While there is considerable controversy over the therapeutic mechanisms of systematic desensitization (see Chapter 6), not even psychodynamically oriented therapists dispute the efficacy of the overall treatment package.

Aside from its applied utility as an effective treatment technique, systematic desensitization has been invaluable in two other ways. First, it has provided a treatment prototype for the laboratory investigation of the maintenance, measurement, and modification of fear. Second, as an effective, easily replicable treatment method, it serves both as a standard for evaluating new behavior techniques and as a testing ground for conflicting theoretical positions.

Among such new techniques, *reinforced practice* consists of graded practice in approaching the phobic situation, feedback of improvement, social reinforcement for progress, and instructions designed to inculcate expectancies of therapeutic gain. Reinforced practice has been shown to be effective in treating a wide variety of fear. *Participant modeling* is a technique that resembles reinforced practice, since both treatments effect change by modifying avoidance behavior directly. With participant modeling, the therapist first models the appropriate behavior, assists the individual in the task of approaching the feared situation or object, and then gradually withdraws this supportive function. Comparative outcome studies have shown that participant modeling is more effective than systematic desensitization and symbolic modeling. Finally, *flooding* is a method in which the client is exposed to the maximum-intensity fear-producing situation directly without any graduated approach. Such exposure might be symbolic or in vivo. Real-life exposure has been shown to be more effective than imaginal presentation of fearful stimuli unless the client engages in self-directed in vivo exposure between therapy sessions.

While most intensively researched, anxiety and phobic reactions are not the only focus of treatment within the neurotic disorders. The charge is often made that while behavior therapy may be appropriate for simple phobias, it is inapplicable to more complex and difficult types of neurotic disorders. However, the evidence—much of it the product of recent and ongoing research—indicates that this view is no longer tenable. Thus complex phobias, such as agoraphobia, have been successfully treated with behavior therapy, often with as much success as in the modification of simpler phobias.

As another example of the broad applicability and robustness of behavior therapy, let us consider the treatment of obsessive-compulsive disorders. There is little disagreement that obsessive-compulsive disorders are among the most severe and disabling of disorders. They have remained notoriously resistant to treatment of any kind, and they provide a searching and decisive testing ground for potentially effective therapies. As in other areas, the behavioral treatment literature shows a definite progression toward the development of increasingly refined and more effective therapeutic techniques.

Thus, after methods such as imaginal desensitization proved to be largely ineffective, in vivo flooding (nonreinforced exposure) and response prevention were developed. Response prevention involves helping the patient to stop engaging in ritualistic behaviors when exposed to the conditions that normally elicit such behavior. Unlike desensitization, these newer methods have shown considerable success. Steady progress of this sort is reassuring, since it is consistent with the nature of scientific advances. It suggests that the positive results obtained are less likely to be a flash in the pan produced by fadlike enthusiasm for a new treatment.

Much of the evidence for the efficacy of the behavioral treatment of obsessive-compulsive disorders rests on uncontrolled or only partially controlled clinical trials. Illustrating the former, Meyer, Levy, and Schnurer (1974) reported that 10 of 15 severely disturbed patients who were treated with response prevention and in vivo exposure were either totally free of their compulsive behaviors or markedly improved according to blind, independent assessments. Foa and Goldstein (in press) treated 21 patients with a combination of in vivo exposure and strict implementation of response prevention procedures. After an intensive two-week therapy program, two-thirds of the patients were asymptomatic. While such results are remarkably encouraging, they are of course far from conclusive.

However, in a controlled investigation of severe, hospitalized patients, Marks, Hodgson, and Rachman (1975) showed that in vivo flooding and modeling treatments with self-directed response prevention were significantly more effective than a relaxation control treatment in substantially reducing compulsive rituals. Although the nature of the placebo control treatment employed could have been methodologically more stringent, these findings are all the more significant since treatment evaluation consisted of actual behavior avoidance tests in addition to patients' self-reports and independent assessments of outcome. At a two-year follow-up evaluation, 14 patients were judged to be much improved, one patient improved, and five unchanged. The efficacy of the specific behavioral methods is difficult to determine at the two-year follow-up, since many patients had received booster sessions or other treatment after their discharge from the hospital. For 11 patients, family members were actively involved in treatment. As discussed in Chapter 6, lasting treatment effects with complex and difficult disorders will be achieved largely to the extent that deliberate steps are taken to ensure the maintenance of treatment-produced change. A well-controlled treatment study by Mills et al. (1973) found dramatic reductions in the compulsive behaviors of five patients. By using single-case experimental designs, these investigators demonstrated that their gratifying results could be directly attributed to the specific response prevention method they employed and not to other nonspecific treatment influences.

To sum up, these encouraging findings on the use of in vivo exposure and response prevention methods have been replicated by independent clinical investigators in several different countries. In many instances improvements in specific compulsive rituals have resulted in more general changes in sexual, social, and work-related functioning. Finally, there is tentative evidence that these treatment methods can be carried out by treatment staff other than psychiatrists or clinical psychologists (for a more detailed analysis of the evidence, see Rachman and Hodgson, 1978). Few controlled studies on the modification of obsessional states unaccompanied by compulsive behaviors have been conducted. Other neurotic disorders treated with behavioral techniques include hysterical reactions, neurotic depression, and psychophysiological disorders; in each of these cases, a clinical experimental literature demonstrating the efficacy of behavior therapy is emerging.

Sexual Dysfunction and Deviance

In addition to a number of procedures designed specifically for sexual disorders, many of the techniques described in the previous section have been used in the treatment of these problems. Perhaps the most dramatic demonstration of the efficacy of the direct behavioral treatment of sexual dysfunction has been Masters and Johnson's (1970) two-week rapid therapy program (see Chapter 6 for a more detailed discussion of this work). Behavior therapy has also shown promise in treating several forms of sexual deviance, including homosexuality, transvestism, exhibitionism, fetishism, and even transsexualism. Commonly employed methods include electrical aversion conditioning, aversive behavioral rehearsal, covert sensitization, and self-control techniques.

Marital Discord

Many reports have demonstrated the use of behavior therapy technqiues to reduce marital conflict and to increase specific positive interactions in individual couples. Partners are helped in identifying specific problem areas, providing feedback to their spouses, negotiating constructively in conflict situations, and expressing a positive reciprocal relationship. Typically, treatment involves feedback and instructions from the therapist, modeling of appropriate communications, and behavioral rehearsal.

Most investigations have studied couples whose marriages are not seriously disturbed (even not disturbed at all), have assessed outcome on measures that do not reflect improvements of marital interaction in specific problem areas, or have failed to use control groups to evaluate the contribution of treatment.

Addictive Behaviors

Most commonly treated addictive behaviors include alcoholism, cigarette smoking, and to a lesser degree drug addiction. (Overeating, occasionally included as an addictive disorder, is considered in Chapter 6.) The behavioral treatment of problem drinking has developed from the early, somewhat simplistic use of aversion conditioning to complex and sophisticated multifaceted treatment programs that take into account virtually all of the controlling variables. Techniques that have been applied include electrical aversion conditioning, which has not been shown to be effective, and chemical aversion using emetine, which has been insufficiently tested. Operant procedures within institutional settings have been particularly successful in modifying patterns of excessive alcohol consumption. These procedures have also been successful in treating alcoholics. Other behavioral treatment methods have included behavioral family counseling (including assertiveness training and contingency contracting) and blood alcohol discrimination combined with discriminated aversion conditioning or differential reinforcement. Despite these findings, much work remains to be done before we can be sure that behavior therapy is a useful approach to this complex and difficult behavior problem.

Cigarette smoking has been treated primarily with self-control procedures and aversion conditioning such as rapid smoking. The results—with some exceptions—have been limited to dramatic reductions in cigarette smoking during treatment followed by a progressive return to near-pretreatment smoking levels over the course of a one-year followup. Several behavioral methods, including aversion conditioning, desensitization, and contingency contracting, have been applied to drug addiction. However, controlled outcome studies of the efficacy of behavioral treatment methods for drug addiction are completely lacking.

Psychotic Disorders

Behavior modification programs for psychotic patients have focused on circumscribed behaviors that may have contributed to the diagnosis. Such programs with psychiatric patients have usually used techniques based on operant conditioning methods. Patients may receive reinforcing or, less commonly, punishing consequences for their behaviors in a psychiatric ward. Most applications have been to chronic schizophrenic patients, usually in state institutions. However, programs have been effective with adult patients diagnosed as suffering from organic or acute psychoses and with adolescent or child psychotic patients.

The specific behaviors that have received attention include self-care and ward behaviors, delusions, incoherent speech, social withdrawal, and aggressive behavior. Programs have also effectively developed community-relevant behaviors (e.g., group decision making, seeking job interviews, procuring employment, and attending social functions) while patients have lived in facilities such as halfway houses, community mental health centers, and day treatment programs.

Numerous studies have addressed communication behaviors ranging from rudimentary skills to complex forms of social interaction. Speech has been reinstated in mute chronic psychiatric patients; for individuals who were already speaking, reinforcement techniques have been effective in increasing behaviors ranging from simple greeting responses on the ward to conversation with staff or fellow patients. Occasionally, contingencies are devised to increase communication in group therapy sessions or group activities.

Developing social interaction has extended beyond verbal skills. Several studies have developed such behaviors as speaking up, describing one's own feelings, making eye contact with others, asking questions of others to stimulate their reactions, and so on. Modeling, incentives, role-playing feedback, and instructions have been combined to effect these changes systematically.

The results of operant programs with psychotic patients have been impressive. Improvements in such areas as psychotic behaviors, aggressive and assaultive acts, social interaction, and communication skills have been associated with increased discharge and reduced readmission rates relative to routine ward care and other treatment procedures. For example, a large-scale project completed by Paul and Lentz (1977) compared an operantly based treatment treatment program for chronic psychiatric patients with milieu therapy and routine hospital care. The operant program demonstrated marked superiority over the other procedures both on specific measures within the hospital and up to one and one-half years after patients had been placed in the community. These results are consistent with other controlled investigations on the treatment of psychiatric patients in the hospital, suggesting that the behavioral approach has a clear place in the rehabilitation of the psychotic patient.

Child Disorders

Children with problems varying in type and severity have been treated from the earliest days of behavior therapy. Treatment programs have addressed problems ranging from circumscribed habit disorders in children whose behaviors are otherwise "normal" to multiple responses of children who suffer all-encompassing excesses, deficits, or bizarre behavior patterns (e.g., autism). Conduct problems, including such behaviors as aggressive acts, truancy, theft, and noncompliance with adults, have been among the behaviors treated. The severity of the problem treated varies tremendously. One type of conduct problem viewed by many as distinct from simple deportment problems is labeled hyperactivity. Hyperactivity has been used to denote behaviors such as constant activity, aggression, running around, failure to sit still or to attend to a task, and gross motor activity. Hyperactive behaviors have been controlled by reinforcing activity incompatible with constant movement. For example, in a classroom program, Ayllon, Layman, and Kandel (1975) decreased motor behaviors, disruptive noise, and similar behaviors and enhanced the academic performance of children diagnosed as chronically hyperactive. The children received one of two treatments, drug therapy (methylphenidate) or token reinforcement, over the course of the investigation. In the token reinforcement program, points later exchangeable for various rewards were administered for completing academic assignments. Both drug and reinforcement treatments decreased hyperactive behaviors. However, the drug tended to hinder whereas the reinforcement program accelerated academic performance. The success of behavioral treatments of hyperactivity in this and other investigations has made them a viable alternative to drug treatment for this common disorder.

Delinquency is a major conduct problem treated in institutions and in home-style community-based behavioral programs. One of the most elaborate and well-investigated treatment models involves adjudicated children who participate in a family-style facility with a few other delinquent youths. A highly trained couple, "teaching parents," administer an incentive system that encompasses virtually all aspects of everyday life. Programs have typically focused on altering academic behaviors and social interaction as well as self-care. Evidence suggests that recidivism and school performance after treatment may be enhanced through intensive behavioral treatment relative to traditional institutional care or probation.

Childhood psychoses, characterized by such symptoms as lack of affect, performance of repetitive and self-stimulatory behavior, severe withdrawal, and muteness or echolalia, have also been treated with behavioral techniques. Self-stimulatory and self-destructive behavior such as biting and head-banging have been eliminated with aversive procedures. Positive behaviors have been developed to improve language and speech, play, social interaction and responsiveness, and basic academic skills.

One of the most effectively treated childhood problems has been enuresis. The well-known bell-and-pad method has produced improvement rates greater than 80 percent in many reports. Toileting accidents have been effectively altered with other behavioral procedures as well.

Mental Retardation

Behavior modification with the mentally retarded has treated a wide range of behaviors that reflects the diversity of age groups, levels of retardation, and treatment settings found among the retarded. Most attention has been devoted to enhancing self-care, language, and social behavior. Although operant conditioning techniques are used most frequently, other techniques, such as modeling, role playing, and rehearsal, have been used as well, either alone or in conjunction with operant techniques.

Self-care behaviors represent a particularly important focus in programs with the retarded because fundamental care skills frequently are unlearned or performed very inconsistently. Self-care responses include toileting, feeding, dressing, grooming, exercising, and personal hygiene.

Toilet training has received the greatest attention, and it well illustrates the approach and overall goal of developing self-care skills. Effective treatment methods have been developed that include frequent and immediate reinforcement for dry pants and for urinating correctly, a large number of trials to practice appropriate toileting, imitation and manual guidance to help initiate behavior, symbolic rehearsal of the desired behavior, and other techniques. The procedure has effectively eliminated toileting accidents with both institutionalized retarded as well as normal children in a relatively brief period of time (e.g., in less than a day; Azrin and Foxx, 1974). Follow-up data suggest that the gains are maintained several months after treatment (Foxx and Azrin, 1973).

Additional Applications

The applications of behavior modification so far discussed are to populations and disorders that have been traditionally included in psychiatry and clinical psychology. Interestingly, behavior modification has contributed to several other areas as well.

Medical and Psychophysiological Applications

Behavior therapy has been applied to many medical and psychophysiological disorders, an area referred to as "behavioral medicine." Most prominent has been the use of biofeedback to alter diverse physiological responses, for example, cardiovascular responses such as heart rate and blood pressure. Several reports, mostly of normal subjects, have shown that cardiovascular functions can be controlled, although the magnitude of change is small and of unclear clinical relevance. Additional reports have suggested that biofeedback may be useful in altering epileptic seizures, tension and migraine headaches, partial loss of muscle control, tics, functional diarrhea, incontinence, sexual arousal, and vaginismus. Although select demonstrations have been dramatic, controlled investigations showing the specific role of biofeedback for most of these clinical problems are lacking.

An alternative technique involving muscular relaxation, with or without the use of biofeedback, has been used to treat essential hypertension (e.g., Jacob, Kraemer, and Agras, 1977; Shapiro, Mainardi, and Surwit, 1977), tension headaches, and insomnia. Initial controlled studies in these conditions appear to demonstrate the efficacy of this rather simple procedure. Another behavioral intervention, contingency management, has been used to treat chronic pain. Pain-related behaviors, such as spending time out of bed, grimacing, moaning, verbal complaints, walking in a guarded or protective manner, reclining or sitting to ease pain, and relying on medication, have been altered by reinforcing activity and physical exercise and by decreasing attention and delivery of medication for complaints (e.g., Fordyce et al., 1973).

Beyond the problems already mentioned, behavioral techniques have been applied to asthma, epilepsy, spasmodic torticollis, ruminative vomiting, diarrhea and constipation, dermatitis, drooling, posture, anorexia nervosa, persistent coughing, sneezing, vomiting, and other medical problems. Adhering to medication schedules, increasing fluid intake, using prosthetic devices, and exercising would be included in the area of adherence.

Adult Offenders

Behavior modification programs have been implemented for adult criminal offenders in various settings, ranging from minimal security facilities to maximum security prisons. Some programs have been designed explicitly to manage prisoners whose behavior is not otherwise controlled. Other programs have been designed not only to manage behavior in prison but to decrease subsequent inmate recidivism. Each of these goals has been met by developing reinforcement programs. Typically, the behaviors developed include self-care, getting up on time, attending activities, performing academic tasks or maintenance jobs in prison, or acquiring vocational skills. Programs have consistently demonstrated the marked effects of reinforcement on inmate behaviors. However, the results following release have not been encouraging. At best, these programs have resulted in only a slight or temporary decrease in recidivism.

The Aged

A few inroads have been made with behavior modification of the aged in settings such as nursing homes and geriatric wards in hospitals. The general focus of such programs is to increase physical activity and social interaction. In institutional settings, physical activity has been encouraged by providing incentives such as tokens or special activities for physical exertion (e.g., using an exercycle or walking). Attention and praise have increased such behaviors as initiating conversation or responding verbally to others. Some programs have focused on increasing purposeful activity in general, such as reading, writing, using recreational materials, and so on.

Educational Applications

Behavior modification techniques have been widely applied in educational settings for diverse age groups and student populations. Populations included in the educational applications are normal, conduct-problem, mentally retarded, delinquent, and emotionally disturbed children and adolescents as well as normal college students. The bulk of the applications in education have been with children, particularly at the preschool and elementary levels. Programs have emphasized deportment so that students are trained to work quietly, to attend to the teacher or task, not to disrupt class or argue, to comply with instructions, and in general to adhere to classroom rules that are designed to facilitate work. Typically, students receive reinforcing consequences in the form of approval, tokens, feedback, or special privileges.

In addition to deportment, academic performance has also been altered in many classroom applications. Behaviors such as accuracy in reading, arithmetic, handwriting, and spelling are included in many programs. In general, research has consistently shown that academic performance is readily altered as a function of incentives for assignment completion in the classroom. Interestingly, the gains in academic skills can be seen on achievement and intelligence test performance.

At the college level, behavioral techniques have been extended by providing students with self-paced or personalized instruction. Course materials are structured so that students receive constant feedback for performance and proceed at their own rate as they master individual units. The area of personalized instruction has developed on its own although it has direct roots in behavioral interventions.

Social and Community Extensions of Behavior Modification

Behavior modification has been extended to a wide range of social and community problems, an area referred to generally as "behavioral community psychology." Diverse problems have been attacked with behavioral techniques, including pollution control and energy conservation, job performance and unemployment, community self-government, racial integration, and others. For example, multifaceted treatment packages have been used in training individuals to obtain and pursue job leads, to rehearse and role-play behaviors that are likely to enhance success at job interviews (e.g., dressing and grooming, and preparing a resume), to expand job interests, and other behaviors. The interventions have been shown to enhance job procurement. Considerable attention has been directed toward enhancing on-the-job performance. Incentives ranging from feedback and social approval to small monetary rewards have increased efficiency at work and the number of jobs completed, and have reduced absenteeism, tardiness, and cash shortages.

General Comments

In this rather dizzying overview of the efficacy of behavior therapy, we have only highlighted the major areas of application and the most-used behavioral intervention procedures. Such a review helps convey to the reader the breadth of application and some of the treatment accomplishments. However, the vast literature encompassed by the different problem areas is not adequately conveyed. Nevertheless, the overview samples some of the *content* areas of behavior therapy. Perhaps as important, if not more so, are the methodological characteristics of behavioral treatment research. Subsequent chapters outline the methodological characteristics of behavioral research and the type of programmatic research needed to establish empirically based treatment. However, before considering these issues, we will review the type of outcome research that has been the hallmark of psychotherapy research.

3

Conventional Clinical Outcome Research

As we have seen in the preceding chapters, specificity is a distinctive feature of all facets of behavior therapy. It characterizes the assessment of presenting problems, the design and implementation of treatment interventions, and the evaluation of therapeutic outcomes. As a result, outcome research on the efficacy of behavioral methods has been directed toward the evaluation of specific techniques applied to particular problems. Especially common have been comparisons of the relative efficacy of different well-specified procedures for a given problem.

Conventional clinical outcome research has been quite different both in design and execution. Here the emphasis has been on the application of a single general psychotherapeutic approach to a range of diverse disorders. In contrast to the search for specific treatment-outcome relationships, which has dominated outcome research in behavior therapy, conventional psychotherapy outcome studies have investigated global treatment methods applied to heterogeneous disorders. Two fundamental questions concerning outcome have typically been addressed by this conventional research strategy. First, does

psychotherapy produce greater improvement than
no therapy at all? Second, are some forms of therapy
superior to others? With the advent of behavior
therapy, this latter question has usually involved less
than dispassionate debates over the relative merits of
psychotherapy and behavior therapy. Another aspect
of conventional outcome research has been the fact
that individual comparative studies have often had
the aura of "crucial" experiments intended to resolve
once and for all which approach is better. Depending
on the outcome of a given study, the results may be
interpreted as the definitive evidence of treatment
efficacy.

The conventional outcome research strategy is illustrated by the much publicized study of Sloane et
al. (1975). In short, 90 adult patients at an outpatient
clinic were randomly assigned to one of three treatment conditions after being matched for sex and severity of disturbance. The patients were relatively
well educated, young, and mainly white, with neurotic and personality problems. Severely disturbed
patients were deliberately excluded. The three treatment conditions were psychoanalytically oriented
psychotherapy conducted by three experienced
therapists of this theoretical persuasion, behavior
therapy conducted by three equally experienced
therapists, and a waiting-list control group. Patients
in the last group received identical pretreatment
assessment interviews, were promised therapy after
four months, and were contacted periodically to ascertain their status and remind them of forthcoming
treatment. Weekly therapy sessions lasted for four
months, followed by a posttreatment evaluation and
an eight-month follow-up. The dependent measures
consisted of ratings of three primary "symptoms"
(target behaviors)—estimates of work, social, and
sexual adjustment derived from a structured in-

terview—and an overall rating of improvement. These ratings were made by the therapist, by the patient, by an independent assessor, and by an informant who was a close friend or relative of the patient. The results showed that in terms of the target symptoms, roughly 50 percent of the control group and 80 percent of the behavior therapy and psychotherapy groups were considered improved or recovered. Behavior therapy produced significant improvement in both work and social adjustment, whereas psychotherapy resulted in only marginal improvement in work. Moreover, behavior therapy was significantly superior to the other groups on the global rating of improvement. At follow-up there were no overall differences among the three groups on any of the dependent measures. However, when differences between treatments were tested by individual *t* tests, the group receiving behavior therapy (unlike the group receiving psychotherapy) showed significantly greater improvement on target behaviors than did the control group. This latter difference is difficult to interpret, however, because the three groups received different amounts of treatment during the follow-up phase of the study.

Unquestionably, this study is the finest example of its kind. Yet it nicely exemplifies the problems of this type of evaluation as well, problems that will be discussed later, after placing this study within a broader perspective of thinking about therapy outcome.

The Sloane et al. (1975) study is one of several recent publications that have contributed to a reevaluation of treatment outcome research. Particularly noteworthy among these publications are two influential reviews of the therapy outcome literature by Luborsky, Singer, and Luborsky (1975) and Smith and Glass (1977). These reviewers concluded that psychotherapy is more effective than no treatment and that different treatment approaches, including behavior therapy, are equally efficacious.

Obviously, acceptance of the conclusions reached on the basis of these reviews of treatment outcome research would have major implications for future research and clinical training in this country. Accordingly, Kazdin and Wilson (1978) scrutinized the conclusions arrived at in the Luborsky, Singer, and Luborsky (1975) and Smith and Glass (1977) reviews in the context of a comprehensive analysis of over 70 comparative clinical outcome studies. All studies were reviewed in which behavioral treatment had been compared either with a specific alternative treatment or with what is typically described as routine hospital treatment. Luborsky, Singer, and Luborsky excluded "the huge literature specifically on habit disorders (e.g., addiction and bed-wetting)" and studies that used "student volunteers" as opposed to "bona fide patients" in "bona fide treatment." In contrast, Kazdin and Wilson's evaluative review encompassed comparative studies across the range of behavior disorders, including neurotic and psychotic disorders, sexual dysfunction and deviance, addictive behaviors, delinquency, and childhood disorders. Unlike Smith and Glass, they evaluated only published studies. Moreover, instead of totally disregarding the adequacy and comparability of individual studies, Kazdin and Wilson emphasized the methodological pros and cons of each study.

Summary Findings from Comparative Treatment Studies

The overriding impression from reviewing this literature is the paucity of studies that are sufficiently well controlled to allow unequivocal interpretations of the findings. Basic shortcomings in design and measurement are evident in the vast majority of studies. Many are completely uninterpretable and convey no useful information. Yet it is apparent that despite the seriously flawed nature of the studies reviewed by Kazdin and Wilson (1978), conclusions are being drawn from this data base that may have a major impact on both future research and clinical practice. The present discussion distills some overall findings from the heterogeneous data pool evaluated by Kazdin and Wilson and compares these findings with the conclusions reached by previous reviews of the comparative outcome literature.

- *Not a single comparison showed behavior therapy to be inferior to psychotherapy.* On the contrary, most studies showed that behavior therapy was either marginally or significantly more effective than the alternative treatment.

- *No evidence of symptom substitution following behavior therapy was obtained,* even in studies explicitly designed to uncover negative side effects. Typical of the findings in this respect is the comment by Sloane et al. (1977, p. 100) that

not a single patient whose original problems had substantially improved reported new symptoms cropping up. On the contrary, assessors had the informal impression that when a patient's primary symptoms improved, he often spontaneously reported improvement of other minor difficulties.

- *Behavior therapy is capable of producing broadly based treatment effects on specific target behaviors and related measures of general psychological functioning.* A frequently voiced speculation is that behavior therapy might have greater effects on symptom-outcome measures than on more important or fundamental processes related to general adjustment. This suggestion has reflected the traditional view that behavior therapy is best regarded as a limited and relatively superficial form of treatment that may be useful as an adjunct to conventional psychotherapy. The available data renders this notion untenable.

• *Behavior therapy is far more applicable to the full range of psychological disorders than traditional psychotherapy.* In the Sloane et al. (1975) study, for example, behavior therapy appeared to be more effective than psychotherapy, particularly with the more complex problems in the more severely disturbed patients. This led Sloane et al. (1975, p. 226) to emphasize that "behavior therapy is clearly a *generally* useful treatment." This finding of greater applicability and relevance of behavior therapy stands in marked contrast to the once held view that its usefulness was limited to the treatment of monosymptomatic fears and simple habits.

In a fashion not atypical of conventional appraisals of the outcome literature, Luborsky, Singer, and Luborsky (1975) claimed to have reviewed those studies consisting of "the general run of patient samples who seek psychotherapy" (p. 1006). However, their analysis was restricted to predominantly adult neurotic patients who would generally be considered to have the most favorable therapeutic prognosis. Thus, they excluded all childhood disorders and a wide range of common adult problems, including sexual deviance, addictive disorders, and psychotic disturbances. As such, the studies they reviewed are not representative of the full spectrum of patients for whom psychological treatment is appropriate. A comprehensive assessment of the efficacy of psychological treatment methods must include those patients with problems other than neurotic or mild personality disorders. A major advantage of behavior therapy is that it has been applied to a wide range of different problems. As we saw in the preceding chapter, aside from conventional psychiatric disorders, important applications have been made in education, medical care, and environmental and social problems. Many of the problems that have been addressed by behavior therapists had either formerly received only perfunctory attention or had been beyond the purview of traditional psychotherapy.

To summarize, the treatment outcome literature shows that behavior therapy is frequently more effective than alternative psychotherapeutic methods. Behavior therapy has yet to be shown to be inferior to any such method. Furthermore, behavioral methods are demonstrably more applicable to a much broader range of human problems than verbal psychotherapy, and there is clear evidence of broad-gauged treatment effects across specific target behaviors as well as more general measures of personal, social, and vocational adjustment.

Conceptual and Methodological Problems

Conventional therapy evaluation has consisted primarily of ill-defined treatments that are evaluated with relatively global measures of therapy outcome. Scientific advances both within psychology and in other areas are usually characterized by increasing specificity in the types of questions asked and the answers sought. Psychotherapy outcome research has yet to advance in this respect. This can be readily seen in the manner of assessing therapeutic outcome and in the nonanalytic fashion of evaluating treatments. In essence, conventional comparative outcome research is an attempt to answer the general question of whether one form of treatment (e.g., psychoanalytically oriented psychotherapy) is more effective than an alternative approach (e.g., behavior therapy). Yet this is the wrong question to ask, for it is ultimately unanswerable. The remainder of this chapter briefly reviews why this is so. Conceptual and methodological arguments are offered that dictate fundamental revisions in thinking about evaluation of treatment outcome. The following chapters outline more appropriate directions for future outcome research.

Global Approaches Versus
Specific Treatment Methods

Comparative treatment outcome research has suffered from the tendency to contrast global and usually ill-defined treatment approaches with one another. Thus something called *psychotherapy* is compared with something labeled *behavior therapy.* There are several problems with this strategy.

Repeating the observation of previous commentators on therapy outcome research, Kazdin and Wilson (1978, p. 106) pointed out that

there is no "psychotherapy" to which other approaches can be compared in any general sense. There are only different methods of psychotherapy. The same point applies to behavior therapy. There is no "behavior therapy" in the sense of a specific technique that could be compared to another technique. There are several different techniques that collectively can be referred to as behavior therapy.

Many behavior therapy techniques are based on different assumptions and therapeutic procedures, as indicated in Chapter 1. Nonetheless, evaluations of comparative outcome research almost inevitably focus on comparing the global entities of psychotherapy and behavior therapy as though they were uniform and homogeneous treatment methods.

In their analysis, for example, Luborsky, Singer, and Luborsky (1975) attempted to justify their comparative evaluation of behavior therapy and psychotherapy by claiming that different behavioral treatment techniques do not differ from each other in terms of relative efficacy. This claim is manifestly false. There exists unequivocal evidence that some behavioral treatment methods are significantly more effective than others. For example, performance-based procedures such as participant modeling are superior to techniques that rely on imaginal (e.g., systematic desensitization) or vicarious (e.g., symbolic modeling) sources of behavior change in the treatment of problems (cf. Bandura, 1977a, 1977b; Leitenberg, 1979). In vivo flooding or exposure methods are demonstrably more effective with obsessive-compulsive disorders than treatment methods that rely on verbal or imaginal induction procedures (Rachman and Hodgson, 1978). Sex therapists have found that treatment is facilitated to the extent that therapeutic prescriptions are carried out by the patient in vivo (Masters and Johnson, 1970), and depression appears to be most effectively treated by psychological methods that use performance-based operations to modify negative thought patterns (Beck, 1976).

Evaluations of behavior therapy are particularly vulnerable to distortion if differentially effective techniques are not distinguished. It is the nature of behavior therapy as an applied science to test existing

methods on an ongoing basis, to modify and refine
them, and to develop more efficient and effective
methods. This problem of comparing ill-defined
global approaches without differentiating among
specific techniques confounds most of the conventional comparative outcome literature. For example,
in comparing "behavior therapy" to psychotherapy," Luborsky, Singer, and Luborsky (1975) based
their conclusions on studies that essentially evaluated the use of imaginal systematic desensitization. If anything, that survey was an analysis of the
effects of systematic desensitization in arbitrarily
selected circumstances. Irrespective of the adequacy
of such an analysis—and there are numerous
shortcomings, as Kazdin and Wilson (1978) pointed
out—it is clear that there are now behavioral treatment techniques other than systematic desensitization that are more effective in many instances. A
questionable evaluation of systematic desensitization
cannot pass for a comprehensive evaluation of the
multifaceted nature of contemporary behavior
therapy.

Comparative outcome studies require contrasting, well-specified treatments. The degree of specificity of the techniques determines in part the
extent to which a meaningful comparative study can
be conducted. It makes little sense to contrast techniques with ill-defined components. The specification is essential so that one can experimentally evaluate whether different treatments were conducted
properly and were distinct from each other on process measures. The more that procedural differences
between contrasting treatments are blurred, the more
difficult it is to interpret outcome results, whether
there are differences or not. Replication also depends
on having operationally defined procedures that can

be restated and implemented by investigators un-
familiar with the original research.

Assessment of Therapeutic Outcome

The most glaring inadequacy of conventional comparative outcome research has been the failure to
obtain satisfactory measures of treatment effects.
Assessment has consisted almost exclusively of qualitative and subjective judgments without the necessary quantitative and objective measures of outcome.
Typically, treatment effects have been evaluated in
terms of judgments about whether the client is
"cured," "markedly improved," or "unchanged." Conceptually, the problem has been that traditional
assumptions about personality assessment have
influenced the types of outcome measures employed
and also their interpretation. Traditional views of
personality assessment make the assumption that
there are generalized traits that determine the
client's behavior across different situations and over
time. Assessment of these traits purportedly enables
one to predict the client's functioning over widely differing circumstances. These personality traits are inferred from extremely limited samples of the client's
behavior, e.g., behavior during a structured clinical
interview. Direct observation of the client's actual behavior in real-life settings is largely ignored.

Given the nature of these assumptions about abnormal behavior and personality, treatment outcome
measures have been essentially limited to standard
personality tests, such as the Rorschach, the Min-
nesota Multiphasic Personality Inventory, and others.
However, the evidence indicates that clinical judgments of personality structures made on the basis of

personality tests are neither valid nor useful (Mischel, 1973; Peterson, 1968). Aside from personality tests, the standard outcome measure in conventional treatment research has been global clinical ratings of the patient on the basis of a clinical interview. The therapist's own ratings are obviously susceptible to bias, as are the patient's self-ratings of improvement. As a result, an independent assessor, who ideally is blind to the type of treatment the patient has received, may be used. It is extremely difficult to maintain the blind, however. In a few instances a further effort is made to obtain ratings of the patient's psychological functioning from a close friend or relative who can observe the patient in the natural environment. The Sloane et al. (1975) study, for example, included all four sources of ratings—therapist, patient, independent assessor, and an associate of the patient.

Some of the difficulties in relying on clinical ratings are illustrated by the Sloane et al. findings. The correlations among the four types of raters were extremely low. The problems with unreliable clinical ratings are summarized by Bandura (1969, p. 458):

Conflicting data of this sort are not at all surprising as long as they are not erroneously considered as measures of behavior outcome but are understood instead as differences between therapists' judgmental responses (which rarely correlate perfectly with clients' actual behavior functioning). Indeed, one would expect diminishing correspondence between actual behavior and subjective ratings as one moves from objective measures of clients' behavior to their own self-assessments, from clients' verbal reports of performance changes to therapists' judgments of improvement, [to] therapists' inferences based on client's self-reports to information that happens to get recorded in case notes, and from case notes of undetermined reliability to retrospective global ratings made by still another set of judges who never had any contact with the client.

Comprehensive assessment of therapeutic outcome will necessarily include specific behavioral measures. There are several reasons for this. First, recent conceptualizations of personality assessment have emphasized that clients are best described and understood by determining what they think, feel, and do in specific life situations. Mischel (1973, p. 265) summarized this view of personality assessment in the following manner:

> The focus shifts from attempting to compare and generalize about what different individuals are like to an assessment of what they *do*—behaviorally and cognitively—in relationship to the psychological conditions in which they do it. The focus shifts from describing situation-free people with broad adjectives to analyzing the specific interactions between conditions and the cognitions and behaviors of interest.

Direct assessment of actual samples of behavior in relation to the conditions under which it occurs provides the most relevant information about therapeutic outcome.

Second, behavioral measures are usually more discriminating than global clinical ratings in revealing treatment effects. Many studies have demonstrated important differences in objective behavioral measures where subjective ratings have indicated no evidence of differential treatment effects (cf. Kazdin and Wilson, 1978).

Third, specific behavorial measures are less subject to distortion and unintentional bias on the part of the assessor than more indirect measures that rely on clinical judgment, subjective self-report, or questionnaire responses (cf. Ciminero, 1977).

A major contribution of behavior therapy to the evaluation of therapy outcome has been the development of a wide range of measurement strategies for the assessment and modification of various disorders. Examples of these innovations in the objective measurement of psychological change are the following: behavioral measures of phobic avoidance and compulsive rituals, reliable and valid coding systems for direct behavioral observation of diverse behaviors across different situations, measures of blood alcohol concentration and free operant drinking rates in seminaturalistic settings with alcoholics, audio- and videotaping to secure samples of behavior as it occurs in the problem situation, psychophysiological monitoring systems for anxiety and sexual problems, stabilometer chairs to measure hyperactivity, and urine alarm systems and electric potty chairs (cf. Ciminero, Calhoun, and Adams, 1977).

Adequate assessment of treatment outcome will necessarily require multiple objective and subjective measures. Traditional psychodynamic approaches have deemphasized the importance of direct behavioral measures of change because of their preoccupation with underlying (usually unconscious) personality dynamics. By definition, the latter have to be inferred from overt symptoms. Partly as a result of the rejection of this psychodynamic model, early behavioral approaches concentrated almost exclusively on direct measures of observable behavior. Important subjective measures, such as the patient's self-report of what he or she was feeling or thinking about a situation, were largely ignored or relegated to secondary significance. This single-minded reliance on overt behavior was initially fostered by the philosophical tenets of a strict operant conditioning or radical behaviorist approach, which regards subjective experience as irrelevant or epiphenomenal. However, as noted in Chapter 1, the conceptual bases of behavior therapy have broadened considerably, and measurement strategies have become more comprehensive and sophisticated.

Consider the treatment of anxiety-related disorders. It is now clear that measures of three response systems—avoidance behavior, physiological arousal, and self-report—are necessary. The correlations among these systems are often low. Thus, simply measuring one dimension might miss important changes in the other two. Moreover, there is evidence that these response systems may change at different speeds and be differentially reactive to different treatment methods. The same considerations hold true for other problem areas, such as sexual disorders and depression. Some therapeutic techniques are concerned with a particular dimension of psychological functioning (e.g., self-report of feelings) rather than other dimensions (e.g., overt performances in everyday life). Different problems seen in therapy can be measured across different modalities. Depending on the problem, these modalities may be assessed with different priorities.

The introduction of multiple objective and subjective measurements will allow increasingly more refined and discriminating evaluations of the relative efficacy of different treatment methods. However, there are broader issues relevant to the evaluation of treatment outcome that go beyond specific measurement. The broader criteria for evaluating therapeutic change include the efficiency, cost and consumer evaluation of treatment. These matters are discussed in the following chapter.

Conceptually, most conventional outcome research has been influenced by the psychodynamic or quasi-disease model of psychological disturbances. In this model, clinical disorders are considered to be a function of intrapsychic conflicts. If internal conflicts are resolved through therapy, the person is said to be cured. A recurrence of the disorder is referred to as a relapse. Both cure and relapse are qualitative concepts that have tended to discourage the analysis of specific psychosocial variables that maintain treatment-produced improvement. Specifically, they tend to ignore or downgrade the influence of the social environment on the client's behavior following therapy.

Within a behavioral model, most abnormal behavior is seen as a function of antecedent and consequent environmental events and cognitive mediating processes that may vary in different situations, in different people, and often at different times in the same person. Behavior is neither a product of autonomous internal forces nor a simple function of external environmental contingencies. Psychological functioning involves a reciprocal interaction between a person's behavior and the environment; the person is both the agent and the object of environmental influence. In this analysis, maintenance will depend on a number of factors, including the problem being treated and the circumstances under which it occurs.

From a behavioral perspective, outcome evaluation must distinguish among the initial induction of therapeutic change, its transfer to the natural environment, and its maintenance over time. It is important to distinguish among these different phases of treatment since they appear to be governed by different variables and require different intervention strategies. Generalized behavior change, for example, should not be expected unless specific steps have been taken to produce generalization. Several strategies have been demonstrated to facilitate generalization of treatment-produced improvement.

Similarly, as Kazdin and Wilson (1978, p. 132) noted:

A given treatment might produce highly significant improvement at posttreatment compared to appropriate comparative control groups, but show no superiority at a subsequent follow-up owing to the dissipation of the initial therapeutic effect over time. It would be premature to conclude that such a treatment method is ineffective; a more specific analysis may indicate that it is effective in inducing change, but fails to maintain change. It may be that by complementing the treatment method with strategies designed to facilitate maintenance of change, long-term improvement may be effected. Within this expanded framework it may be that a specific treatment technique and a specific maintenance method are both necessary although neither may be sufficient for durable therapeutic change.

In short, it is inappropriate to use follow-up information as the sole criterion for a dichotomous, all-or-nothing judgment about the success or failure of treatment. Even without the long-term follow-up data of treatment efficacy, a method that produced an initial effect may represent a useful starting point for the design of a more enduring treatment. This would seem particularly true in cases where no other treatment has proven effective.

Implications for Conventional Evaluations of Treatment Outcome Studies

The preceding discussion illustrates the many conceptual and methodological difficulties in the conventional approach to therapy outcome evaluation. The inescapable conclusion is that the vast majority

of conventional comparative outcome studies contribute little or no useful information. Nonetheless,
these methodologically marred studies continue to
be evaluated in a summary, qualitative manner and
entered into the numbers game to determine which
arbitrarily defined treatment approach works best.
This is usually achieved by compiling balance sheets
or box scores in which different studies are cate-
gorized and the resulting totals used to pick the
winner. However, the fact remains that no aggregate
set of such findings is more compelling than the
methodological adequacy and interpretability of the
individual studies of which they are comprised. To
be blunt, twice nothing is still nothing.

A brief analysis will show how the difficulties in
making sense out of individual comparative treatment outcome studies are compounded by the fash-
ionable practice of comparing groups of studies. The
practice of comparing groups of diverse comparative
studies is well illustrated by Luborsky, Singer, and
Luborsky's (1975) well-known review. Using a dichotomous measurement criterion, statistically significant versus nonsignificant, the results of various
treatment outcomes are indiscriminately summed
across different studies and represented as three
distinct categories—"better than," "worse than," and
"no different than" an alternative therapeutic approach. This is the box-score approach. As an alternative, Smith and Glass (1977) proposed "meta-
analysis." The basic unit of meta-analysis is an "effect
size," defined as the mean difference between the
treated and control subjects divided by the standard
deviation of the control group. In their analysis of
therapy outcome studies, Smith and Glass calculated
effect sizes for every type of outcome measure reported in the literature. Thus they mixed together 830

effect sizes from 375 studies. Meta-analysis provides a more discriminating means of quantifying how different features of studies relate to their measured effects. However, no matter how sophisticated the statistical meta-analysis of outcome, the findings are only as good as the quality of the original data. One of the consequences of lumping studies together is that the cardinal tenet of specificity of assessment, treatment, and evaluation is violated. Comparisons among alternative approaches that are obscure within individual studies become still more obtuse.

Both the box-score and meta-analysis strategies inevitably obscure treatment effects by collapsing findings from methodologically inadequate studies using ill-defined treatment methods, heterogeneous clients and clinical problems, and nondiscriminating, noncomparable outcome measures. Statistical adjustments, no matter how sophisticated, cannot overcome these fundamental problems. As Eysenck (1976) noted, borrowing a phrase from the vernacular of computer technology, "Garbage in, garbage out." In an attempt to justify their meta-analysis, Smith and Glass (1977) argued that "all outcome measures [are] more or less related to 'well-being' and so at a general level are comparable." However, research on personality assessment has shown that specific measures of psychological functioning are necessary, since they cannot be assumed to be comparable and may vary across different procedures or problems.

As pointed out earlier, Luborsky, Singer, and Luborsky (1975) were obliged to regard all behaviorial methods as equally effective in their box-score analysis. This assumption is unwarranted. In Smith and Glass's (1977) meta-analysis, different behavioral techniques are said to differ in efficacy, but the specific claims made in this regard are questionable. These authors concluded that systematic densitization is superior to implosive therapy. However, the evidence is quite clear that flooding is at least as effective if not more so than systematic desensitization in the treatment of phobias and especially in the case of obsessive-compulsive disorders. In view of the now huge but uneven quality of the literature on these behavioral techniques, it is not surprising that reviewers who fail to sort out the good from the bad arrive at misleading conclusions.

In the box-score strategy, equal weight is given to different studies despite the heterogeneity of treatment variables and the lack of standardized evaluation criteria. This results in a form of majority rule, in which several poorly designed studies are given more weight than a single well-controlled one. Democratic processes have little place in scientific analysis. Also, there is the question of whether "tie scores," i.e., the absence of significant differences between treatments, should be assigned the same weight as comparisons in which one treatment is significantly superior to another. It must be remembered that the null hypothesis cannot be proved. The demonstration of a statistically significant difference means more than a failure to show a difference. A problem always exists in interpreting negative results. In order to draw any meaningful conclusions from negative findings, it is imperative to consider the possibility that the lack of differential treatment effects is simply the result of inadequate methodology or a poorly conducted study. This parsimonious explanation of the failure to find differential treatment effects is particularly plausible in view of the numerous methodological inadequacies in the conventional comparative outcome studies reviewed above.

4

Alternative Strategies for Therapy Research

Advances in therapy will require a methodological approach that rejects the limitations of conventional outcome research. Evaluation of defined treatments with relatively global measures of outcome must give way to pointed questions about well-specified interventions. These questions need to be answered empirically and with a degree of specificity that is only beginning to be invoked in treatment evaluation. Evaluation of treatment requires many different research approaches, which are differentially useful in evaluating particular treatments and in answering the range of relevant questions related to outcome. The present chapter develops the methodological approaches required to overcome many of the inadequacies of conventional outcome research that were discussed in the last chapter.

Assessment of Therapeutic Outcome

Many of the problems with conventional outcome research can be traced directly to the use of faulty assessment procedures. The use of single measures, often global in nature, obscures the conclusions that can be made about treatment effects. Yet, outcome assessment methods can be criticized for more than their lack of specificity. Therapy outcome traditionally has been conceptualized in a narrow fashion. Many significant dimensions that might be included in the evaluation of treatment have been entirely neglected.

For clinical research, a major, if not *the* major, criterion for evaluating treatment is the importance of the improvement effected in the client, that is, whether improvement enhances the client's everyday functioning. The question is simply: "Did therapy ameliorate the problem for which the patient sought treatment?" This question does not merely refer to categorizing patients as "much improved" or "very much improved"; rather, the extent to which treatment restores adequate or acceptable levels of functioning must be assessed directly. In many ways, evaluating treatment in light of the *importance* of the therapeutic changes seems to be a more appropriate criterion than the statistical comparison of group differences.

The problem with a simple comparison of group differences is that such a comparison averages the amount of change across all clients within each treatment group. Obviously, the average (mean) change of patients may have no counterpart in reality, and it is therefore important to look beyond the mean effect to the impact on the individual. Thus the proportion of clients who reach a particular preset criterion of improvement might be reported. Selecting a treatment that produces improvements in the largest number of clients maximizes the probability that a given client will be favorably affected.

In contrast, selecting a treatment that produces the greatest average change may not improve the largest number of clients.

The primary criterion for change is improvement in the specific problem for which the client entered therapy. However, the breadth and nature of changes beyond this particular focus are also important. Related to the breadth of therapeutic change are the side effects of treatment. Conceivably, two treatment techniques might be equally effective in altering a client's problem. However, side effects might differ enough to recommend one treatment over the other.

The relative paucity of follow-up data in clinical research makes the long-term effects of many techniques a matter of speculation. Debates over the relative effects of different treatments are usually based on immediate treatment effects. It is quite possible that a treatment may show greater improvement at posttreatment assessment but also a more rapid decline of therapeutic change during follow-up than another treatment. Long-term follow-up assessment is essential to evaluate the relative effects of different treatments.

The cost-effectiveness of psychological treatment is also important. Assuming that different techniques are equally effective on a particular outcome measure, the rapidity with which these results are achieved is an important consideration. Obviously, a technique that reaches a specified level of improvement in a shorter period of time is preferable. For example, the psychodynamic approach has traditionally fostered the notion that treatment must be intense and protracted. An alternative treatment need not be more effective than psychodynamic therapy; it simply must show that the same magnitude of change can be achieved more quickly.

Aside from the amount of time required to administer treatment, efficiency can be measured by how treatment is administered; for example, work in groups is more efficient than work with individuals. In addition, the extent to which a technique can be widely disseminated is also a measure of efficiency. Thus a technique that can be widely disseminated but is only moderately effective may have greater impact on client care than a technique that is more effective but less easily disseminated.

One of the most efficient ways to disseminate treatment is through bibliotherapy, or self-help manuals. Of course, the usefulness of such programs depends on their effectiveness. At present few such programs have the benefit of empirical support, and some can be criticized for prescribing clinically unsound procedures. However, even if a self-administered program is less effective than a therapist-administered procedure, its use may still be indicated on the grounds of cost-effectiveness and its greater ease in disseminating.

Several different costs are important in evaluating therapy techniques. One such cost, which is rarely discussed, is the amount of professional training required of the therapist. Traditionally, becoming a therapist, whether within psychiatry or psychology, entails lengthy and expensive training. However, untrained or moderately trained individuals frequently do just as well as professionals in effecting change in particular problems.

Consumer evaluation of therapy has also been conspicuously neglected in therapy outcome research. Different treatments for a given problem may not be equally acceptable to prospective clients. Presumably the acceptability of treatment is influenced by the cost considerations mentioned above. However, even effective treatments may not be acceptable to clients if specific aspects of the procedures are objectionable.

It would seem premature to make definitive claims about the relative efficacy or utility of different treatments before a broad evaluation of therapy outcome has been made. Quite possibly treatments will fare differently across diverse outcome criteria; thus, the superiority of one technique may be limited to a few criteria. The treatment of choice for a given patient may vary according to the outcome criterion best suited to the individual client's problem.

Although follow-up is an essential criterion in evaluating therapy, it warrants additional consideration because of the neglect of long-term effects. Indeed, a major limitation of both psychotherapy and behavior therapy research is the lack of follow-up data. The severity of the problem within behavior therapy was noted by Keeley, Shemberg, and Carbonell (1976), who sampled two years of research (1972 — 1973) in three behavior modification journals to assess how frequently follow-up data were gathered. Although their data were restricted to applications of operant conditioning techniques, the results are instructive. Only 12 percent of the articles examined long-term follow-up (defined as assessment at least six months after the termination of treatment). Many of the studies included merely relied on self-report assessment at follow-up. Thus, questions could be raised about the evidence for actual changes in target behaviors that were not observed directly.

Although the studies sampled by Keeley, Shemberg, and Carbonell (1976) are now several years old, the picture has probably not changed. Very few studies have assessed long-term effects of treatment on behavioral measures outside the treatment setting. Collecting follow-up data is beset with a host of problems that need not be described here. The problem of subject attrition alone is enough to discourage most investigators. However, follow-up data are of such importance that they should be collected routinely.

The need for follow-up data is a perennial problem for any therapeutic or treatment technique. However, it is especially important for behavior therapy. In several areas of behavior modification applied to specific problems (e.g., phobias) or intervention techniques (e.g., applications of reinforcement), research demonstrates that therapeutic changes can be effected. The prospect of effective treatment in many areas does not seem as distant as it did years ago, when basic questions about the efficacy of therapy were first posed. Demonstrations that changes can be achieved in treatment make the issue of the durability of such changes especially salient.

A related reason for stressing the importance of follow-up is the pattern of results in areas where such data are available. Observation has often shown that changes during treatment have little or no relation to follow-up performance. This has been more of a problem in some treatment areas than in others. For example, with behaviors such as overeating and cigarette smoking, treatment effects have been demonstrated in several studies; yet follow-up data have suggested that the effects are transient. Similarly, interventions with conduct-problem children in such settings as the classroom or home frequently show loss of therapeutic gains as soon as treatment is terminated.

Even with the sparse evidence available, it is clear that treatment effects are usually not maintained after the intervention has been terminated and the client has left the treatment setting. Specific provisions may be needed to ensure that the gains achieved during treatment are sustained. Behavior therapy has concentrated heavily on the technology of behavior change. Yet, the technology of change may differ from the technology involved in maintain-ing these changes. In different areas of behavioral treatment, investigators have developed specific interventions that can be added to the basic treatment approach to extend the durability of therapeutic change. Concerted research efforts should be made in the immediate future to further the development and refinement of effective strategies for maintaining behavior change.

Analogue Therapy Studies

The evaluation of therapeutic outcome has been facilitated by posing specific questions, and, as we have seen, behavioral assessment has contributed to this specificity relative to traditional outcome research. Another equally significant contribution has been the reliance on well-controlled laboratory studies to tease out the components of treatment contributing to a successful outcome.

Of course, the most direct means of addressing questions about the efficacy of treatment is to investigate treatment as it is ordinarily practiced in the clinic. This means studying treatment with actual clients and therapists. In the conduct of such research, clients who come for treatment are assigned to appropriate treatment and control groups, and assessment devices are administered to evaluate the

results of treatment. Although these basic requirements can be stated easily, to meet them requires a
Herculean effort in the face of nearly insurmountable
obstacles. A host of practical problems, such as recruiting experienced therapists for the project, keeping clients in the project, ethical obstacles, such as
withholding treatment and assigning patients to
control groups, can make clinicial research difficult
if not impossible and often, even if completed, uninterpretable.

One solution to this problem is to evaluate
treatment under conditions analogous to those obtaining in the clinic. Such research has been referred
to as "analogue." An analogue study usually focuses
on a carefully defined research question under well-
controlled conditions. The purpose of the investigation is to illuminate a particular process or to study
an intervention that may be of importance in actual
treatment. The ultimate goal of analogue research is
to reveal empirical relationships that can be generalized to treatment settings.

An important issue in the therapy literature is
the extent to which analogue studies contribute to
the understanding of therapeutic processes and outcome in clinical settings. It is generally acknowledged
that such studies provide an important link in extrapolating from basic laboratory research to therapy.
Analogue studies allow careful experimental control
by studying circumscribed and well-defined behaviors and by minimizing sources of variances that
might otherwise obscure the effects of treatment.
Thus, subjects can be selected with similar target
problems and similar subject and demographic variables. Similarly, therapists can be selected for homogeneity of training interests and experience. In
addition, control groups not easily used in clinical

situations can be easily employed in laboratory conditions where client treatment is not the highest priority.

The problem of generalizing results can be illustrated by the analogue research on relatively mild fears, which have been exploited in behavior modification. Many behavioral treatments, such as desensitization and flooding, have been explored with college students who have mild fears of small animals, such as harmless snakes. Often such students have been recruited for an experiment with the external incentive of course credit. These subjects were not motivated to obtain treatment for a personal problem of pressing concern. Major concerns have been voiced about the generality of such research to clinical situations. The issue is whether results from these "treatment" studies can be extended to clients with more generalized problems of greater severity. This concern is justified. Recent research has shown that college students' fears of small animals typically habituate more quickly in the presence of the anxiety-provoking stimulus and are more influenced by suggestion than are fears in social situations.

In the clinical literature, therapy investigations are viewed either as analogue or nonanalogue research. Unfortunately, such dichotomizing may obscure the interpretation of research findings. First, the distinction tends to overlook the inherent limitations (and analogue nature) of *all* clinical research, including studies conducted in clinical situations with patient populations. Second, and more important, the categorization does not provide clear guidelines to distinguish among analogue studies.

All psychotherapy and behavior therapy research is analogue research insofar as it constructs a situation in which the phenomenon of interest can be studied. Although the experimental version of the phenomenon may resemble the naturally occurring phenomenon to varying degrees, in an important sense it is only an analogue. Even when therapeutic research is conducted in a clinical situation, it is only an analogue of actual treatment. Thus the ethics of clinical research require that all subjects be fully informed that they are participating in a research project and are being exposed to contrived arrangements. The use of pretreatment assessment devices, screening procedures, and careful arrangements that keep intake workers, therapists, and assessors "blind" all contribute to the experimental nature of the investigation and move it away from the usual conditions of clinical practice.

The assessment of behavior with psychological measures makes an investigation an analogue in an important sense. It is not the responses on psychological measures or therapist ratings per se that are of interest but rather the construct assumed to be represented by these measures. The measures used in research are of interest because they may reflect or relate to changes occurring in the natural environment in the client's ordinary circumstances. Yet, the measured responses are only an analogue of the responses and situations of direct interest.

Viewing all therapy research as an analogue to clinical practice, presumably the situation to which one would like to generalize, has important implications for conceptualizing and evaluating treatment research. Initially, it is essential to keep in mind that investigators are interested in extrapolating research findings to some area, problem, setting, or subject population that is itself not studied directly. The possibility exists always that the extrapolation is not justified. The difference between the clinical situation and an experiment might be precisely along dimensions that restrict generalization. *A major implication of this view is that it is not only fruitless but also counterproductive to speak of analogue versus nonanalogue or clinical research.*

In evaluating therapy research, there are two important questions. First, to what extent do the conditions resemble the situation of interest? Second, to what extent are departures from the clinical situation relevant to extrapolating the results? Studies may depart from the clinical situation along several dimensions. These include the target problem, the population studied, the manner of recruiting subjects or clients or of motivating the subjects for treatment, characteristics of the therapist, the set and expectancies of the client, instructions about the nature of treatment and its effects, the variation of treatment and its departure from clinical practice, the assessment measures, the context in which the measures are administered, and so on.

The generality of an investigation depends on how an investigation compares with the clinical situation with respect to these and similar dimensions. The task for evaluating *any* therapeutic outcome study—whether arbitrarily designated as analogue or not—depends on where it falls on each continuum. More importantly, generalizability of the results depends on how the dimension relates to treatment efficacy.

It is usually assumed that departure from the clinical situation on a particular dimension decreases the generality of the results. With many dimensions, this may be so. Yet, with other dimensions the laboratory results might still be quite applicable to the clinical setting. For example, departure from a clinical situation on some dimensions may make behavior

change more difficult to achieve. In these cases behavior change in the nonclinical situation might even
be a more convincing demonstration of a treatment
effect than application in the clinical situation.

A problem in therapy research is that analogue
studies have been rejected on the grounds that, by
their very nature, they provide a weak test of the relationship between a treatment variable and client
change in the clinical situation. Yet, this is not necessarily the case. The relation between a laboratory-
based study and a clinical situation for a given dimension is itself an area of research. Research is
needed to investigate the influence of departures
from the clinical situation along various dimensions
and the implications of such departures for generalizing results to clinical situations. Comparisons of
varying degrees of resemblance of research to the
clinical situation for a given dimension can reveal
whether departure from the clinical situation at-
tenuates, enhances, or has no effect on treatment.

Single-Case Experimental Methodology

Research conducted under well-controlled laboratory
conditions can greatly expand the types of question
that can be addressed. The laboratory permits dissec-
tion of various treatments and implementation of
control conditions not permitted in clinical settings.
Yet the clinical situation also provides an important
opportunity for experimental evaluation of treatment
within the single case.

To date, evaluation of therapy has been based
largely on group research and the examination of the

average change among many clients. An alternative approach is to investigate the individual case directly. Developing and evaluating treatments at the case level is not an endorsement of the traditional case study. Although the case study may provide insights and hypotheses about treatment, it characteristically relies on anecdotal information and impressionistic accounts. Studying the individual case does not necessarily mean that experimental evaluation of treatment must be sacrificed. Recent clinical research has demonstrated that the single case can be evaluated with much experimental rigor. Thus single-case experimentation has been used widely to evaluate behavioral treatments for diverse therapeutic problems, including delusions and hallucinations, avoidance behaviors, alcohol consumption, overeating, hyperactivity, autistic behaviors, and so on. However, single-case methodology need not be restricted to a specific type of treatment or model of behavior change.

Characteristics of Single-Case
Experimental Methodology

Single-case experimental designs refer to several different methods of investigating treatment with one individual. Although the designs can be used with more than one individual and even with very large groups, they are uniquely suited for evaluating the individual client in treatment. Different designs are available that are suited to a particular question about treatment and to the constraints of the clinical situation. The present situation can only highlight general characteristics of these designs. (For a more detailed account, see Hersen and Barlow, 1976).

The general characteristics of single-case experimental designs are the observation of overt behavior, continuous assessment of behavior, the use of data to make decisions about treatment, and specific criteria for assessing the reliability and importance of therapeutic change. First, in single-case designs, problem behavior is observed directly either in the situation of interest or in simulated circumstances where the behavior is sampled under laboratory conditions. Objective measures of overt behavior refer to direct observations of what the client does or does not do. The objectivity of the measurement strategy refers to the fact that observers can independently record the behavior reliably. Such observations, while not free from bias, have been shown to be much less amenable to assessment artifacts than are more global evaluative measures. The objectivity derives from focusing on observable behaviors; thus, the observations are based on publicly available information.

A second characteristic is the continuous measurement of behavior. Performance of the client is examined prior to treatment, usually on a daily basis. Assessment of the problem behavior or therapeutic focus continues through treatment. In the individual case, such assessment provides immediate information about whether treatment is having the desired effects. One needs to know during treatment if it is accomplishing or approaching the original treatment goal. Continuous assessment of behavior allows the therapist to make data-based decisions about treatment. Treatment can be continued, intensified, or completely altered on the basis of the data.

The third characteristic of the single-case experimental approach refers to both the experimental and the therapeutic criteria for evaluating treatment. The experimental criterion refers to demonstrating that reliable changes in behavior have resulted from treatment. This criterion is satisfied by assessing whether treatment is associated with change, whether the pattern of change makes other threats to the internal validity of the demonstration implausible, and whether the effects obtained would have been predicted from the data without the intervention.

The therapeutic criterion refers to evaluating the clinical importance of behavior change. This criterion evaluates the magnitude of performance and the importance of this change for the individual's day-to-day functioning. The clinical importance of the change has been assessed by determining whether treatment alters how the client is viewed by others in his or her everyday environment and whether treatment brings the client's behavior within acceptable or normative levels of performance. Acceptable or normative levels of performance are defined empirically by observing individuals who are functioning adequately in the natural environment.

Limitations of Single-Case
Experimental Methodology

Although single-case methodology offers important advantages for clinical research, it is advocated here as a supplement to traditional treatment research. Any research methodology has its own limitations and weaknesses. The single-case method, for example, is not particularly strong in revealing client characteristics that may interact with specific treatments. Examination of subject variables requires the group research that has characterized traditional psychotherapy evaluation. Also, the results of single-case demonstrations provide no hint of the applicability of the findings to other cases. Another problem with single-case research is that it is not well suited to investigating strategies for maintaining behavior. Although single-case designs can demonstrate that therapeutic improvements are maintained, it is not always possible to show unequivocally that a particular intervention was responsible for sustained improvements.

One problem that has received considerable discussion is the failure of single-case designs to suggest the extent to which findings can be generalized. One answer to this problem is the replication of single-case experiments. Additional tests of the efficacy of a single method can be conducted. If the treatment is demonstrably effective with all clients, the results are easily interpretable. However, if the results are mixed, the investigator cannot know whether the method is of limited utility or whether one of a number of possible causes of interclient variability was responsible.

Single-case experimental designs have been hailed as the means of merging the roles of the scientist and the practitioner. However, the ethical, practical, and methodological difficulties inherent in establishing cause-effect relationships using single-subject methodology resemble those using between-group outcome research. If the client is receiving therapy, many of the critical requirements of single-case experimental designs are difficult if not impossible to meet. In essence, all such designs necessitate baseline observations, holding certain conditions constant at different times and intervening selectively in a limited manner at any one point. This often conflicts with the priority in service delivery settings to treat the client's problems in as effective and efficient a manner as possible.

Despite these limitations, the single-case experimental method has added much to therapy research and often nicely complements the more traditional between-group design.

5

Additional Therapy Research Strategies

As we have seen, the expansion of assessment methods, the use of analogue or laboratory research, and the advent of the single-case experimental design provide a broader and more analytic base for developing treatment than traditional outcome research has afforded. But, in addition, a broader range of questions about therapy must be considered. Several strategies for evaluating therapy exist. Each strategy addresses a specific question about treatment, has different requirements and limitations, and reflects the different aspects of outcome research needed to elaborate information about a given treatment (Kazdin, 1979).

Treatment Evaluation Strategies

Treatment Package Strategy

With the treatment package strategy the effects of a particular treatment are determined. Treatment may consist of several components distinguishable both on conceptual and operational grounds; for example, participant modeling includes specific therapeutic instructions, modeling, guided practice, *in vivo* exposure, self-observation, and positive reinforcement. A treatment package approach is often the first used to evaluate therapy for determining if treatment alters the problem for which it was designed. To answer this question, the minimal comparison conditions are treatment and no-treatment control conditions.

Evaluation of the efficacy of a single therapeutic technique (e.g., systematic desensitization) in the treatment of a particular problem is an example of *technique-oriented* outcome research. The relatively restricted conditions of controlled research of this nature necessitate that all clients be treated in the same way with the same technique. In other words, different clients are treated as if they were a homogeneous group. Yet, even within the limited classification of phobias, the variables that maintain phobic behavior may vary from one individual to another. To the extent that multiple variables determine a clinical problem, a multifaceted treatment program is required to modify them. Clinical practice requires a *problem-oriented* approach, in which multiple treatment techniques are tailored to an individual client's particular problem.

Given the problem-oriented approach, a complex, multifaceted treatment may be necessary to produce clinical change. With the emphasis on helping clients, many ingredients may comprise treatment, including some that are unnecessary and perhaps even ineffective. Yet, at this stage of research the extra ingredients are not too important. If the entire treatment package with all its distinguishable components changes behavior, then the researcher can begin to scrutinize particular components.

The importance of the package approach to clinical research cannot be overestimated. In clinical work, the highest priority is given to effecting maximal behavior change. The applied commitment of clinical research makes changing behavior of more immediate import than analyzing the reasons for change. A treatment package approach emphasizes the importance of outcome, whereas the analysis of the components of treatment emphasizes understanding the reasons for the change.

While the priority of producing clinical change often dictates the use of treatment packages consisting of multiple methods, this strategy is not without problems. From the standpoint of treatment evaluation and analysis, it is important to ensure that the program is not so complex and wide ranging that identifying the specific techniques becomes difficult. Similarly, it should not be so diverse that there is difficulty in keeping the program distinct from other therapeutic methods in terms of both concept and practice.

Dismantling Treatment Strategy

The dismantling treatment strategy refers to analyzing the components of a given treatment in order to understand the basis for treatment effects achieved by the overall package. To dismantle a given technique, individual treatment components are eliminated. Comparisons are usually made among groups that receive the entire treatment package or the package minus specific components. Each component may be withheld from some clients and presented in varying degrees across clients. In addition, the separate and combined effects of different components can be evaluated. Differences across groups, depending on the specific design, can suggest whether certain components are necessary and sufficient to effect behavior change and whether specific components produce additive or interactive effects.

The results of a dismantling strategy usually go beyond the implications of conducting treatment and bear upon the theoretical notions that served as a basis for the derivation or explanation of the technique. By dismantling the treatment package, the investigator can determine whether the ingredients thought to be crucial for behavior change are in fact crucial. Research on the technique of systematic desensitization, for example, has thoroughly exploited this strategy. When desensitization was originally proposed, specific ingredients were carefully described as essential for therapeutic change. These included having the client learn a response (e.g., relaxation) to compete with anxiety, preparing a hierarchy of anxiety-provoking situations, and pairing these situations in imagination or in the actual situation with the anxiety-inhibiting response. Dismantling research has evaluated variations of treatment to assess the role of these ingredients. The results have shown that these components can be omitted without loss of treatment effect. The only component that appears important is imagined or overt rehearsal of the response that is to be developed. These findings have had important implications for the theory about the mechanisms responsible for behavior change in desensitization.

Constructive Treatment Strategy

In contrast, within the constructive treatment strategy a treatment package is developed by adding components to enhance outcome. With this approach, the investigator begins with a well-circumscribed treatment and adds various ingredients to determine which increase effectiveness. As research continues, effective components are retained and a multicomponent treatment package is constructed. The addition of techniques to the package need not necessarily result from theoretical considerations. Indeed, the characteristic of this approach is in empirically establishing components that, when added to treatment, enhance outcome.

Research in the area of modeling illustrates the constructive treatment approach. Modeling as usually conducted consists of having a client observe someone else perform a particular behavior. Research has demonstrated that modeling effects are enhanced when the client not only observes the model but also engages in the modeled behavior. Further research has shown that adding supplementary performance aids and guided participation components produce still greater therapeutic change.

The advantage of the constructive treatment approach is that it empirically establishes a treatment package. Components that are shown to enhance treatment outcome are added to the basic procedure. As this process continues, the efficacy of the package increases. As a scientific and applied endeavor, clinical psychology has the dual goals of developing treatment and understanding the reasons for its effects. Yet a constructive approach may not necessarily shed light on the mechanisms of behavior change. Research along these lines can proceed empirically so that components are added to treatment without understanding how they operate or interact with other components. Ideally, however, the components added to treatment in a constructive approach would derive from a theoretical context so that the investigator has some guide for determining which components to add.

Parametric Treatment Strategy

As with the constructive treatment strategy, the main purpose of the parametric strategy is to examine dimensions that enhance treatment effects. However, in the constructive strategy, components of treatment are usually added to an existing treatment. The constructive approach usually evaluates the effects of adding *qualitatively* distinct interventions. Indeed, different treatment packages might even be combined in a constructive evaluation approach. In contrast, the parametric strategy usually varies one or more *quantitative* dimensions within an existing treatment package by providing more or less of a given portion of treatment. Thus, parametric investigations have focused on such variables as the amount of treatment and the number, spacing, and duration of individual sessions. With such parametric variations, each of the groups studied might receive the same general treatment.

Parametric research can also vary qualitative aspects of a given treatment. Most therapeutic techniques have many unspecified dimensions. Working within the technique, many aspects can be altered to determine their effect on outcome. For example, in a therapeutic procedure such as modeling, the basic ingredient is observing or imagining someone perform a particular behavior. But the treatment does not specify *who* the model should be (e.g., someone similar or dissimilar to the client) or *how* the model should behave while performing the behavior. Yet each of these factors contributes to treatment effects. Thus, aspects of the treatment may be varied to reveal parameters of treatment that enhance therapeutic change.

The parametric evaluation strategy is useful in many of the same ways as the constructive evaluation strategy. The evaluation of specific treatment parameters can help build an effective treatment strategy. In addition to maximizing treatment outcome, the parametric approach can reveal important information about the theoretical basis of the technique and the mechanisms responsible for change.

Comparative Treatment Strategy

Comparative research usually holds wide interest because theoretical battles over the bases of different therapies ultimately reduce to relative efficacy. As discussed in earlier chapters, premature comparisons of treatment may have clouded the evaluation and interpretation of treatment outcome. The major objection to traditionally conceived comparative research is the comparison of ill-defined omnibus treatment programs with heterogeneous behavior disorders by using unsatisfactory and global outcome measures. Yet the fact that traditional comparative outcome research has been methodologically marred in this manner does not mean that well-controlled comparative studies are not feasible under certain circumstances.

In a successful application of the comparative evaluation strategy, Gelder et al. (1973) compared specific treatment methods (systematic desensitization and flooding) with an attention-placebo control condition in the treatment of phobic disorders. Treatments were carried out by experienced therapists explicitly trained in administering the different methods. An attempt was made to induce a high expectancy of success in half of the subjects by describing the treatment and therapist chosen in very favorable terms and showing them a videotape of a client who had benefited from the treatment they were to receive. Treatment effects were evaluated in terms of measures of behavioral avoidance, blind psychiatric ratings, client self-ratings, physiological responsiveness, and standardized psychological tests. The ability of the control group to elicit expectancies of treatment success comparable to those evoked by the two behavioral methods was assessed directly.

Half the clients were agoraphobics, the other half a mixed group having specific phobias. Agoraphobia is regarded as more difficult to treat than simple phobias. Clients were assigned to treatments and therapists in a factorial design that permitted an analysis of the possible interactions among treatment effects, therapist differences, types of phobia, and levels of expectancy. Treatment duration was 15 weekly sessions, similar to the Sloane et al. (1975) study, with a three-month and six-month follow-up. In short, the Gelder et al. (1973) study was sufficiently well designed and well executed to determine what treatment method has what specific effect on what problem in whom. It provides one methodological model for comparing specific treatment methods with each other and with an interpretable placebo control condition.

Client and Therapist Variation Strategy

So far the discussion of evaluation strategies implies that specific techniques have certain relatively straightforward effects. Little mention has been made of the clients and therapists who are involved in treatment and their influence on therapeutic outcome. The client and therapist variation strategy examines these influences in two ways. Clients and therapists can be selected for specific attributes, or the behavior of therapists can be experimentally manipulated.

Clients might be selected for the study because of differences in age, sex, socioeconomic standing, marital status, education, or personality measures such as introversion-extraversion or suggestibility. Therapist variables have been studied in a similar fashion by looking at such characteristics as therapist training, years of experience, age, interests, various personality traits, and empathy and warmth during the sessions. Finally, particular combinations of client and therapist variables can be examined.

When clients and therapists are classified according to particular subject variables, the main question asked is whether treatment is more or less effective with certain kinds of participants. An interaction of treatment with the characteristics of the client or therapist suggests that treatment is more or less effective depending on the variable used to classify the therapist or the client. Such findings are potentially useful in making decisions about the type of treatment appropriate for clients with certain characteristics.

The client and therapist evaluation strategy also embraces direct manipulation of independent variables rather than merely subject selection. Instead of correlating therapists' attributes (e.g., empathy or warmth) with outcome, these characteristics can be manipulated experimentally. Therapists can behave differently with clients as the dimensions vary.

The selection of clients and therapists according to specific dimensions makes the evaluation of treatment outcome more precise. It is unlikely that answering a simple question such as which treatment produces greater change or which components enhance treatment will be the most productive approach. To such questions must be added stipulations about characteristics of the clients and therapists. The study of variables associated with treatment effects begins to define the boundary conditions of a given technique and the areas where different techniques produce different advantages.

Internal Structure or Process Strategy

The above research strategies refer to what traditionally has been called outcome research. Process research addresses questions that pertain to the transactions between the therapist and client, as well as the type of interactions and their interim effects on client and therapist behavior. Process and outcome research are usually dichotomized. Process research is viewed as the study of activity within the therapy session while treatment is still in process, whereas outcome research evaluates the final effect of treatment. While the distinction holds in certain types of research, it is often profitable to reject the dichotomy, since in-session behavior is actually an interim measure of outcome.

The relevance of the process of change to outcome is often illustrated in single-case experimental designs where assessment of the behaviors of interest are continuous throughout treatment. For example, Bornstein, Bellack, and Hersen (1977) treated withdrawn and shy children with modeling, rehearsal, and feedback. Throughout treatment, progress was assessed on specific measures, including characteristics of speech in role-playing situations, clients' responses to requests, and overall assertiveness. The measures of progress reflect the process of change. Yet these same measures also indicate whether the desired outcome has been achieved at the end of treatment and at follow-up.

Not all research on the processes of therapy can be reinterpreted as an interim measure of outcome. For example, research on the internal structure of therapy may examine aspects of the therapist's behavior over time and is purely a study of internal changes in treatment that says nothing directly about how or what the client is doing. In this kind of research the characteristics of events in treatment are the focus, and they may or may not bear on therapeutic behaviors related to improvement in the client. Rather, the goal is to understand the mechanisms of change and the course of events in therapy.

Research on the internal structure of treatment is presumably most appropriate after the treatment package itself has been proven effective. While the interaction between a therapist and client might be of interest in its own right, selecting therapy for process evaluation would be of dubious value if such treatment was not effective. Internal structure or process research raises questions about techniques rather than treatment problems. However, by isolating particular processes associated with successful outcome, hypotheses can be generated and tested about the essential components of a given treatment. Hence, process and outcome research, even as traditionally conceived, are quite related.

General Comments

The foregoing treatment evaluation strategies address different but complementary questions. The strategy that is most relied on for a given technique may depend on how thoroughly the technique has been investigated. Preliminary research of a therapeutic technique is likely to adopt the package, constructive, or parametric evaluation strategies. After the technique has been shown to be effective in altering a particular problem, it is likely to be evaluated more analytically with dismantling, client-therapist variation, or internal structure strategies. Along with this, investigators will compare the newly established package with techniques claimed to be effective for a particular problem. There tends to be an evolution of the type of research strategy adopted that is suited to the development of the technique. However, this evolution is not fixed. Indeed, a dramatic way to increase visibility of a given technique, long before it has been carefully established in package evaluation research, is to conduct a comparative study. If the technique can be shown to be superior to an existing technique, it is likely to generate a flurry of enthusiasm in the field more quickly than a treatment package evaluation strategy would. Thus, comparative research may be the first strategy adopted. However, comparative research usually requires greater effort than treatment package research in terms of the number of subjects, therapists, and groups needed. Thus, unless there is some preliminary assurance that the new treatment will be fruitful, the extra effort of comparative research might be profitably deferred for later studies.

Another reason for holding comparative questions in abeyance pertains to development of the individual treatments that are to be compared. Early in the development of a given therapeutic technique, the parameters that maximize treatment efficacy are not well known. Research examining parametric variations that maximize treatment effects must precede comparative work. Only then does comparing the new treatment with another treatment that has achieved similar status make sense.

Aside from the status of research for a given technique, the priority of the investigator regarding applied or basic research aims determines which treatment evaluation strategy is adopted. As mentioned earlier, treatment package, constructive, and comparative approaches are likely to be adopted if the primary commitment is applied research. In this context, effecting the greatest change as efficiently as possible is more important than understanding the theoretical basis for the technique or the mechanisms of change. In contrast, within laboratory-based research greater priority can be given to isolating a treatment's effective components. The goals of effecting change and understanding the basis for the change are not incompatible. However, they usually do vary in priority across investigations and treatment evaluation strategies.

Control Groups for Treatment Evaluation

Evaluation of the efficacy of therapy depends on careful experimental control over rival hypotheses that might account for therapeutic change. Several different control conditions can be used depending on the research evaluation strategy and the purpose of the investigation. The range of available control procedures cannot be reviewed here. However, it is useful to briefly discuss two major control conditions—the no-treatment (and waiting-list) control and nonspecific treatment.

No-Treatment and Waiting-List
Control Groups

The design of research for assessing the efficacy of a given treatment usually must include a group that does not receive treatment, in order to determine whether treatment effects greater change than no treatment at all. Methodologically, a no-treatment group controls for several threats to internal validity, such as history, maturation, the effects of repeated assessment, instrument decay, statistical regression, and similar factors that might contribute to or account for change.

In the psychotherapy literature, changes that occur independently of formal treatment are referred to as *spontaneous remission*. Regardless of the reasons for these changes, they must be controlled when evaluating a particular treatment package. Hence, a no-treatment control group is essential unless the level of improvement for a given set of clients can be precisely identified in advance of an investigation.

However, there are both practical and ethical obstacles in using a no-treatment control group. Assigning patients to a no-treatment group is likely to result in high levels of attrition. Clients will seek some form of treatment if it is not provided within the study in which they agree to participate. To avoid this problem, clients are often promised that treatment will be provided after a waiting period, which corresponds to the time required to treat other clients in the study. Such clients constitute what is referred to as a waiting-list control group. A waiting-list control group does *not* allow long-term comparison of treatment and no-treatment groups because the no-treatment group is eventually treated. Hence, the waiting-list control group is only a partial solution.

Aside from the practical problems of using a no-treatment group, there are obvious ethical constraints. When clients seek treatment, it is difficult to justify withholding all attempts at intervention. Even a treatment that may exert little influence can be defended better than no treatment—in part because of the placebo effects associated with any treatment. These difficulties present problems for conducting basic research on the efficacy of a given treatment package. Alternative strategies for evaluating treatment outcome can avoid using a no-treatment group when different treatments or variations of treatment are compared.

Nonspecific Treatment Control Groups

A frequently discussed issue in psychotherapy research is the influence of factors such as the therapist-client relationship, suggestion, client belief in the curative effect of treatment, attending therapy, and similar influences that may contribute to client improvement. Virtually all therapies share such general characteristics as providing a client with a rationale that places their problem into a coherent theoretical framework, engaging in specific procedures designed to ameliorate the problem, an attentive and interested therapist who is committed to the treatment process, and similar factors. The components of treatment such as therapist support, which are not specific to any particular form of therapy, may also contribute to client change. These components have been referred to as "nonspecific treatment factors," and the therapeutic changes resulting from these factors have been referred to as "nonspecific treatment effects."[1]

Nonspecific treatment factors present an obstacle for therapy evaluation whenever investigators wish to attribute the effects of a given treatment to specific ingredients peculiar to a particular therapy. In treatment research, nonspecific effects have been controlled in one of two ways. First, an investigation can include at least two treatment groups as would be done in the dismantling, constructive, comparative, and parametric strategies. Each treatment would include many of the nonspecific treatment factors, such as a rationale about therapy, establishing a therapeutic relationship, and providing several treatment sessions. Hence, any differences between groups would be attributed to specific ingredients of treatment rather than nonspecific treatment effects.

A second and more recent approach toward controlling nonspecific treatment effects is to include a pseudotherapy or attention-placebo group in the investigation. The purpose of this group is to provide all the nonspecific factors of treatment without presenting a veridical therapy procedure. Clients might meet with a therapist and engage in tasks that are considered by the therapist to be therapeutically

---

[1]The term *nonspecific* is an unfortunate one. The many therapeutic factors lumped together under this rubric are quite specific. It is more realistic to propose that although many nonspecific influences still remain to be specified, they are neither intrinsically unspecifiable nor qualitatively very different from other independent variables involved in planned behavior change.

inert. In general, a nonspecific treatment control group is modeled after the placebo control in drug research, in which clients receive an innocuous substance that should not effect direct physiological change. Ethical problems exist in providing treatment that is thought to be inert. In addition there are practical problems. Thus a group receiving an inert treatment may suffer from attrition as clients seek more effective alternatives.

Recent research suggests that nonspecific treatment effects may not be as easily controlled as originally thought. Treatment and nonspecific treatment control conditions have been found to differ in their degree of credibility to the clients and the extent to which they generate clients' expectancies for improvement. Hence, if the investigator wishes to make claims as to why change has occurred or why one treatment works better than another, then differential credibility across alternative treatments must be ruled out as a rival hypothesis.

General Comments

The research strategy and the control conditions used to evaluate treatment must evolve together as the nature of the questions change. In an early stage of research, attention is likely to be given to treatment package or constructive strategies. Control conditions consist of no-treatment or waiting-list groups. As the package is shown to be effective, more analytic work is likely to begin. Dismantling and parametric strategies come to the forefront. The control conditions then include treatment groups that differ in select and often subtle dimensions in order to isolate factors that contribute to or enhance change. Research on the mechanisms of change is extremely important because it helps develop the basis for an effective treatment. The principle, theory, or mechanisms through which treatment attains its effects can be revealed through such analytic work.

Recommendations and Future Directions

As we have seen, traditional therapy research has been relatively restricted in the type of methodology, assessment techniques, and criteria for improvement used and in the unprogrammatic way in which the techniques have been evaluated. In the last two chapters we have suggested that a given treatment technique must and can be evaluated with a broad range of strategies. Different strategies address specific questions about the efficacy of treatment and the relative efficacy of different techniques. There is an evolution of questions and research strategies dictated by the extent to which a technique has been established in the literature. Traditional therapy methods, and to some extent behavior therapy, have not systematically put techniques through the range of questions that the strategies outlined earlier are designed to assess. To be sure, each research strategy has been employed, but a systematic progression from one to another has not always been apparent.

The virtues of between-group research are obvious and need not be reiterated here. Although such research should and will continue, therapy research would benefit from increased use of the single-case experimental methodology. There are several advantages to this approach. First, it provides an empirical and scientific basis for investigating treatment with individual clients. Second, it allows investigation of problems that are not likely to be studied in between-group research. For example, treatment of relatively rare problems cannot be studied in large-scale group investigations. However, these can be carefully studied and treated in each individual case by using single-case experimental designs. Third, the single-case methodology allows effective interventions to be built by adding components to enhance behavior change. In this manner single-subject methodology dovetails with the constructive strategy of treatment development discussed earlier. Conversely, the methodology allows analysis of treatment packages by withdrawing components of treatment to determine essential treatment elements—the single-subject equivalent of the dismantling strategy. Finally, different treatments can be compared for the individual client.

New therapy techniques are often developed from clinical practice. After a clinician discovers an apparently effective procedure, the technique can be evaluated in a between-group design against either a no-treatment control group or alternative treatments. The leap from clinical practice to between-group research is long and may account for some of the unexciting results of many outcome studies and of empirically evaluated therapy in general. Between the clinical application or case study and large-scale between-group evaluation might fall single-case experimental research. The single-case method allows one to subject treatment to rigorous small-scale testing. The constant feedback provided by continuous assessment of behavior allows the investigator to improvise changes as needed to augment the effects of treatment. Repeated single-case application of treatment and demonstration of therapeutic efficacy would in many instances seem to be an appropriate screening device before techniques are subjected to the more expensive and time-consuming between-group investigation.

In addition to single-case experiments, laboratory-based group research is to be strongly encouraged. This research, often rejected as a mere therapy analogue, provides a model for scientific evaluation. Such research allows for careful specification of treatment, which is essential to ensure that the causal agent can be identified once experimentation is completed. Moreover, specification of treatment permits replication of research and treatment by others. Related to this is the needs for precise assessment and evaluation of behavior change and homogeneity of client selection to allow for precise evaluation of the problems and behaviors for which treatment is suited.

Laboratory research permits careful control over treatment. Dimensions that would normally vary can be standardized or controlled. The careful control of laboratory-based research is evident in the types of questions that can be asked. The basic questions about a given treatment and parameters that contribute to its efficacy are difficult if not impossible to answer adequately in a clinical situation. Adequate control strategies to vary subtleties or even to provide major ablations of treatment are rarely possible in the clinic, where research is necessarily subordinate to treatment.

Of course, advocating use of laboratory research does not ignore the application of findings to clinical situations. Yet, it is rare that psychotherapy research can rigorously evaluate the internal validity of a variable without sacrificing external validity and vice versa. This suggests that clear findings need to be established under controlled conditions, replicated, and then evaluated under conditions where less control is possible. *The empirical foundations for behavior therapy and psychotherapy may not derive from the situation in which the techniques are normally used.* Once techniques are evaluated in controlled situations and parameters that contribute to change are assessed, they can be extended and evaluated in less controlled situations.

In addition to direct tests of treatment in the clinical situation, additional bridging work is needed to assess the effect of departures from the clinical situation. As noted earlier, analogue evaluation of treatment does not necessarily limit the generality of the results. The dimensions that do contribute to the generality of laboratory-based findings need to be evaluated. Such research will help establish the relevance and limitations of controlled studies that depart from clinical practice.

6

The Progression of Therapy Research

Although important, improved methodology alone is not enough to ensure progress toward the elusive yet desirable goal of developing effective therapies. As suggested in the previous chapters, attaining this end requires a systematic expansion of knowledge (starting with the generation of new intervention procedures), adequately testing and refining such procedures, and finally implementing them. At each stage of development the research question being posed changes, and the appropriate methodological approach to that question must be taken.

As illustrated in Figure 1, new procedures can be generated from clinical observation or from basic research and theoretical considerations. Once generated, a phase of testing is begun, which leads to controlled comparisons of the short-term effects of the new therapy and culminates in assessment of the maintenance and generalization of the achieved behavior change. At this point implementation begins, either by direct application—if the effects of the new therapy are clearly superior to existing procedures—or by comparison with the most effec-

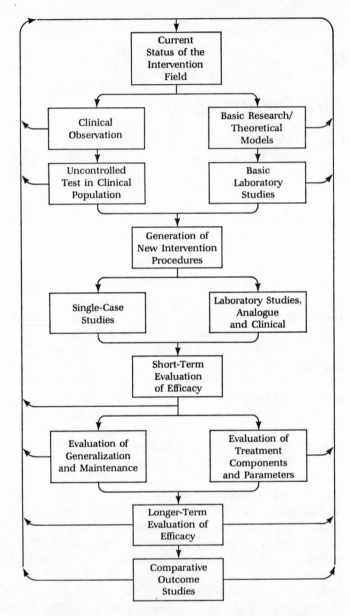

Figure 1. The Flow of Therapeutic Research

tive treatment in common use. But before conducting such a test, several facets of the therapeutic procedure, such as the best way to present the treatment (e.g., in individual or group settings), the level of therapist training required to implement the therapy, and identification of the most effective therapeutic components must be studied experimentally.

The work on phobia will illustrate this progression of research from idea to application. This is a particularly appropriate topic to examine, since it was one of the first problems tackled by behavior therapists and was the subject of that pioneering and influential work *Psychotherapy by Reciprocal Inhibition*, written by Wolpe in 1958. The choice of phobia might be viewed as emphasizing the narrow focus of behavior therapy. Other techniques, such as the token economy or the use of relaxation procedures for certain psychosomatic conditions, could have been chosen, as could other problems, such as depression or childhood autism. However, such areas are less well developed and do not illustrate the progression as well as research on phobia.

Generating a New Therapy

Dissatisfaction with both the theory and the therapeutic results of psychoanalysis, which was at that time the state of the art, led Wolpe (1958) to formulate a new theory of neurosis, "based on modern learning theory," and a new approach to treatment, based both on that theory and the results of a series of animal experiments originally published in 1952. In the animal work, Wolpe produced experimental analogues of neurosis in cats, using strong, inescapable electric shock. He also treated this neurotic behavior by feeding the cats in situations gradually approximating the situation in which shock had been used until no abnormal behavior occurred in the original cage. These observations led Wolpe to formulate a general principle:

If a response antagonistic to anxiety can be made to occur in the presence of anxiety-evolving stimuli so that it is accompanied by a complete or partial suppression of the anxiety responses, the bond between these stimuli and the anxiety responses will be weakened [p. 71].

In the case of the cats, food was hypothesized to produce a parasympathetic response antagonistic to anxiety. However, in the case of humans, Wolpe took a great conceptual leap. He equated muscular relaxation with eating as the response inhibitory to anxiety and an imaginal approach to feared situations with the actual approach used in the animal experiments. Wolpe next applied systematic desensitization to a large number of phobic patients, obtaining promising results; nearly 90 percent of 210 patients were considered to be "cured" or "much improved" after treatment. Thus, desensitization was generated from an appraisal of the status of the intervention field, from theoretical considerations, from basic research, and from clinical observation of the results of the new procedures when applied to phobic patients.

Testing New Therapies

For most new therapies the chain of events would have ended there. Desensitization would have been enthusiastically applied by therapists who espoused the theory and practice. A myriad of therapies, from psychoanalysis to gestalt therapy, attest to this outcome. Why, then, did the field take a different direction? Several factors may account for the enormous surge of research during the next 15 years. First, the procedure of desensitization had been well specified, so that it could be applied by others in a relatively standardized version. This, as we have seen, is in sharp contrast to the procedures of psychoanalytic psychotherapy, which are complex and poorly specified, making replication by other workers almost impossible. This view is shared by workers in the field of psychoanalysis, as demonstrated by the conclusions of Fisher and Greenberg (1977, p. 411) following their detailed review of psychoanalytic theory and practice:

The field [of psychoanalytic therapy] is filled with vagueness, appeals to authority rather than evidence, lack of specificity in the definitions used, and unreliability in the application of techniques and dynamic conceptualization.... It is our conclusion after reading through the literature that a single unified approach to the treatment of patients that can be labeled "psychoanalysis" does not exist.

Which, we would add, makes evaluation impossible.

Second, an objective measure (the behavioral avoidance test) of fearful behavior and phobia was developed in which the ability to approach a feared object or situation was directly observed and measured. Third, a convenient population of snake-fearful subjects was available, which allowed laboratory studies of desensitization. Finally, Wolpe proposed a testable theory concerning the mechanism of desensitization.

Two lines of research rapidly emerged. First, Lazarus (1961), moving beyond Wolpe's uncontrolled clinical series, found in a randomized clinical trial that desensitization administered in a group was superior to group psychotherapy. This pioneering study of short-term efficacy was followed in the next few years by several similar studies, all of which found that desensitization was superior to other therapies. There was, however, a tendency toward less clear-cut results in the treatment of that most disabling condition, agoraphobia. Second, Lazovik and Lang (1960) demonstrated that desensitization was superior to no treatment in snake-fearful subjects, opening the way for further laboratory studies.

The outpouring of well-controlled laboratory studies that followed was directed toward testing the theory of reciprocal inhibition underlying desensitization and toward delineating the components of therapy that were *essential* for success by using dismantling, parametric, and constructive research strategies. Within a few years it became obvious that many elements of desensitization could be removed without greatly impairing the effectiveness of therapy. Thus, pairing relaxation and feared scenes did not seem to be critical for successful outcome, and the arrangement of feared scenes in a graded-approach hierarchy was also found to be unnecessary. Moreover, elements not stressed in the original description of the procedure, such as therapeutic instructions, were evidently important. Systematic desensitization was not an automatic form of conditioning.

Nothing like this had ever occurred in the field of psychotherapy research. Serious questions had been raised about the procedural approach and the underlying theory which was based not on clinical speculation and armchair rhetoric but on empirical findings. Yet the treatment was effective. The major question became, How does systematic desensitization work? Analytic studies examined the necessary and sufficient conditions required. In addition, the question was answered by a search for alternative fear reduction methods, such as shaping, modeling, implosion, and flooding. Here the diversity of the field strongly favored the solution of the problem, for the answer came from both operant and social learning theory approaches and from empirical clinical investigations of new procedures.

It was natural that an operant approach to fear reduction should be one of the first to be considered, since reinforcement had been found useful in enhancing a variety of behaviors. In a series of single-case controlled experiments, Agras, Leitenberg, and Barlow (1968) and their colleagues demonstrated that social reinforcement could be used to reduce agoraphobic behavior. However, in the course of this work, some patients with long-term chronic phobias were found to improve steadily when their phobia was measured directly, which of course necessitated placing them in their feared situations. The first hypothesis tested to account for this improvement was that such patients could observe their progress, either by the amount of time they could spend in the situation, as with claustrophobia, or by how near they could approach a feared object, as in the case of an animal phobia.

In a series of single-case experiments, information feedback was found to be responsible for gains but did not seem to be a particularly powerful agent of behavior change. Thus, the hypothesis that exposure to the feared situation was responsible for the therapeutic effect was finally tested. Again, in controlled single-case experiments, the effect of alternate periods of exposure and nonexposure to the feared situation with careful control procedures to equate for expectancy of therapeutic benefit was tested. Improvement *only* occurred when patients were exposed to their feared situations. Talking about fears and conflicts with no exposure to the actual situation produced little or no benefit.

Meanwhile, laboratory research conducted by Bandura and his colleagues demonstrated the powerful effects of observational learning, and this procedure, termed modeling, was investigated in a series of laboratory experiments. For example, children who were afraid of dogs were found to improve more if they could see another child interact fearlessly with a dog than if they just watched a dog themselves. It soon became clear that watching a live or filmed model produced therapeutic benefits and, finally, that participant modeling was more effective than imaginal modeling and systematic desensitization (Bandura, Blanchard, and Ritter, 1967). This work again suggested that direct exposure to and practice in the feared situation is the most effective approach to the treatment of phobia.

Finally, a series of clinical studies from the Maudsley Hospital and Institute of Psychiatry in London (Marks, 1978), for the most part aimed at determining the short-term effects of various treatments, fleshed out the developing picture. These workers first examined the efficacy of implosive therapy, in which intensely fear-arousing phobic scenes were repeatedly presented, and they then observed the effect of increasingly long periods of practice in the actual phobic situation, which this group termed *flooding*. Although some of this research was marred by the use of global rather than specific measures, the results demonstrated that exposure was superior to both desensitization and implosion, findings that have since been confirmed using behavioral measures.

Thus, evidence from these disparate lines of research converged on one conclusion, that practice in the feared siutation was the most effective way to treat phobia. Procedures such as desensitization, reinforcement, feedback, modeling, prompts, and therapeutic instructions were all effective *insofar as they led to exposure to the phobic situation.* Procedural differences between shaping, participant modeling, and flooding appear to be relatively minor, since some motivational procedure to enhance approach to the phobic object or situation is emphasized. Obviously, the ideal treatment should contain as many procedures to enhance motivation as possible. Thus, not only was the procedure of systematic desensitization replaced by more effective methods for the treatment of phobia, but the original theory was found to be inadequate to account for the experimental findings.

In turn, this stimulated the development of further laboratory work and many alternative theoretical explanations. In particular, Bandura proposed that behavior change procedures strengthen expectations of personal effectiveness, which in turn affect the choice of activities and persistence in pursuing them under adverse circumstances. Expectations of personal effectiveness are considered to be formed by observing one's own performance, observing others, verbal persuasion, and perception of states of physiological arousal. Empirical tests of this hypothesis confirm that various treatment approaches, such as feedback concerning behavior change, lead to changes in self-efficacy. Moreover, measures of self-efficacy seem to predict improvement in behavior rather well. This theory, which may well apply across a variety of behavior change situations, is an important development, demonstrating the interaction be-

tween laboratory experiment and hypothesis forma-
tion, and is, of course, likely to lead to the generation
of new therapeutic procedures.

Although this systematic research effort was
more detailed than any other previous psychotherapy research effort, a glance at Figure 1 reveals
some shortcomings. Little is known about the generalization of improvement from one set of fears
to another, or about improvements of related problems found in phobic patients, such as social disability. In addition, few studies have examined maintenance of therapeutic effects over one or two years,
and not one for as long as five years. Existing studies
of maintenance suggest that we can be relatively op-
timistic about the endurance of therapeutic behavior
change in the phobias, but further work is needed to
confirm this view. Moreover, almost nothing is known
about procedures that might be used to enhance
maintenance, another area of research that needs to
be developed.

Toward Implementation

When a therapeutic procedure with satisfactory
short-term outcome and reasonable maintenance of
effect has been developed, new issues become important (see Figure 1). Some of these issues have been
addressed for the exposure therapies. Thus, aspects
of the delivery of treatment have been systematically
varied, for example, by comparing the results produced by a therapist with those produced by tape
recordings of therapeutic instructions and by comparing the results produced by individual and group

treatment. Therapeutic effect is much diminished when therapy is by tape recording; however, group exposure is as effective as individual treatment, which is an important finding since group treatment saves expensive therapist time and reduces the cost of treatment.

In a similar vein, Marks and his colleagues in London described a program to train nurses to treat phobic and obsessive-compulsive disorders and examined the costs and benefits of such treatment (Marks et al., 1977). Nurse therapists obtained treatment results comparable to those obtained by psychologists and psychiatrists, with the advantage that the nurses required less training time. The benefits of treatment exceeded the costs when improvement continued for more than two years. This was largely the result of three factors: reduced use of treatment facilities after therapy, a reduction of absenteeism from work, and reduced family expenses as a result of enhanced functioning. Factors such as reduced suffering and increased enjoyment of life were not assigned a monetary value and can be regarded as added benefits.

Some other issues have not been examined thoroughly, including a delineation of the characteristics of clients who are likely to respond to treatment and an examination of alternative therapeutic approaches for those who do not do well with the exposure therapies. Finally, no entirely satisfactory long-term study comparing a large number of patients treated by an exposure therapy and by a standard treatment, such as the use of the antidepressant medication imipramine, has been reported. At this level of outcome comparison, as indicated in the previous chapters, both therapies should consist of the ideal treatment form. Thus, an exposure therapy might include the following: imaginal approach to the feared situation, gradual approach to the actual feared situation assisted with modeling and reinforcement, generalization training to the same fear in different situations and to related fears, family involvement to reinforce therapeutic gains, and preparation of both the patient and family to deal with any tendency toward relapse. Also included should be an adequate follow-up and additional treatment as necessary. The cost of each therapy should be measured and the benefits in terms of direct assessment of changes in the target behavior, in related behavior, and in social behavior should be ascertained.

Reality Versus Theory

As we have seen, there are quite large gaps in our knowledge, even when one of the best worked-out therapies is considered, and these areas of ignorance vary with the problem and the therapy used. Since many investigators with differing interests are involved, the development of a new therapeutic procedure is often short-circuited. Therapists will not wait for definitive knowledge to accumulate before applying a new therapy because of the need to provide as effective a service as possible for their clients. Nonetheless, in order to apply a therapy with reasonable certainty of its effects (and complications) and with the greatest cost-effectiveness the critical body of knowledge implied in Figure 1 is required. To illustrate this point further, the development of therapies for eating disorders and for sexual behavior problems will be examined.

Eating Disorders

Obesity

Since obesity is such a widespread problem in affluent societies, it is natural that behavior therapists should have focused on it in the early 1960s. At that time traditional approaches to treatment, such as combinations of diet and psychotherapy, had not proven particularly successful. There was a high dropout rate from such treatment, and only 12 percent of treated clients lost as much as 20 pounds, the vast majority regaining weight after one year. In 1962 Ferster and his colleagues (Ferster, Nurnberger, and Levitt, 1962) suggested a novel treatment approach for obesity, based on the theory and findings of operant psychology and on their clinical observation of the obese. One of their main hypotheses was that the eating behavior of the obese was under powerful stimulus control; that is, their eating was largely controlled by environmental factors such as the sight of food. To correct this, Ferster suggested that eating should take place only when sitting down at a particular distinctively laid table. Thus, eventually only the cues involved in this particular situation would lead to hunger and eating. The second procedure suggested was that the obese should slow their eating behavior by chewing their food more and pausing between bites, thus reducing caloric intake. A further stimulus for providing a new therapy for the obese was the basic experimental work of Schachter (1968), which suggested that the eating behavior of the obese and the nonobese was indeed more under the control of external events in the environment. By changing such events, obese eating behavior and weight might be altered.

In 1967, Stuart published the results of a treatment approach based on these findings in an uncontrolled study of ten patients. Therapy consisted of self-monitoring food intake, teaching stimulus control, slowing eating, reinforcing weight loss, and increasing activity. Of the eight patients completing treatment, all lost more than 25 pounds in one year. These dramatic results immediately stimulated a flurry of research, first demonstrating that the therapeutic package was superior to no treatment and then that it was superior to control procedures of various types, including alternative active treatments such as the combination of psychotherapy and diet. However, there was marked variability in the amount of weight lost by different clients treated in the same program, and the amount of weight lost by the average client was relatively modest—about 11 pounds. Such variability suggests that more must be learned about the different types of obesity, the types of client who will respond to treatment, and the best procedure to use. Nonetheless, in immediate outcome, behavioral approaches appear to be at least as effective as the use of anorectic drugs, such as fenfluramine, and safer to use.

Along with research into the immediate outcome of the behavioral treatment package, a number of investigators have studied the eating behavior of the obese and nonobese. While the results of this work are still unclear, it seems probable that the overweight eat more quickly and chew their food less than the nonobese, thus supporting attempts to change patterns of eating behavior. However, again there is much individual variation, with some of the obese eating like thin individuals, and vice versa.

The variability of response to therapy also led to studies of some of the components of weight-loss programs. Thus stimulus control procedures seem to be an effective and powerful component of treatment, as does reinforcement of weight loss. Moreover, setting short-term rather than long-term goals seems to be a helpful procedure in achieving weight loss. Identification of the critical components of treatment will undoubtedly lead to the development of more effective weight-loss methods.

Thus, short-term efficacy and some of the components of treatment needed for successful weight loss have been identified. But longer-term efficacy is less certain, since only 5 percent of studies report the outcome of treatment after one year. The few studies published suggest that weight loss is reasonably well maintained one year after treatment but that differences between alternative treatment approaches and behavioral approaches tend to disappear on further follow-up. This should not occasion much surprise, since there has been little research into the factors involved in maintaining weight loss, and the small amount of research in this area has produced conflicting results, suggesting that there is much left to learn.

The findings that treatment results are not well maintained and that even the immediate outcome of treatment is more modest than might have been expected from the early work in the field have given rise to some disillusionment with the treatment approach and even to signs that the approach might be abandoned. Such a step would, of course, be premature, since the flow of research beyond immediate outcome has been sluggish. Studies of generalization and maintenance are now needed, as is a continuation of work aimed at identifying the most effective procedures to produce weight loss. Only then can research proceed to the phase of implementation.

Anorexia Nervosa

In contrast to obesity, anorexia nervosa is a rare condition, usually found in adolescent girls who do not eat and hence lose much body weight. This condition is often associated with severe disability, at times resulting in death. The development of a behavioral approach to this condition was stimulated by a case report (Bachrach, Erwin, and Mohr) published in 1965. In this case, eating was fostered by reinforcement, and a moderately successful outcome was reported.

These findings were replicated in small uncontrolled series of patients, suggesting that a successful therapeutic procedure had indeed been isolated. A series of single-case experiments (Agras et al., 1974) confirmed that reinforcement led to weight gain and that feedback for progress and serving large meals were also effective therapeutic procedures. Outcome at one year or more, at least in uncontrolled series of cases, seems to be reasonably favorable. However, no controlled outcome study comparing behavior therapy with other methods has yet appeared. Moreover, no work has appeared on how to treat many of the problems associated with anorexia nervosa, including the interpersonal problems. Thus a start has been made, but so far even the short-term effectiveness must remain in doubt, and much remains to be done before studies of implementation can proceed. Still, it must be emphasized that more is already known about behavioral approaches to anorexia nervosa than about such approaches as psychotherapy, where not a single controlled study exists.

Sex Therapy

Less closely allied to behavior therapy in its origin than treatments for phobia, obesity, and anorexia nervosa, sex therapy sprang directly from the physiological research of Masters and Johnson (1970). Moving from direct observation of the physiology of sex behavior and guided by those observations and clinical experience, Masters and Johnson developed specific approaches to the treatment of such problems as premature ejaculation, frigidity, and impotence.

Like the approach in behavior therapy, the aim was to directly improve sexual performance by carefully shaping the desired behavior and at the same time dealing with interpersonal problems directly related to the sexual disorder. The original therapy seemed to be so superior to prevailing psychotherapeutic approaches that Masters and Johnson proceeded with a large uncontrolled test in a clinical population and found that 81 percent of their clients benefited. At follow-up five years later, nearly all those treated maintained their improvement. But despite these impressive results from uncontrolled work, remarkably few controlled trials of this therapeutic approach have been performed. One recent notable exception found that the Masters and Johnson approach was superior to systematic desensitization and that the use of two therapists, one male and one female, somewhat improved the results. In another controlled study, various behavioral procedures were tailored to each individual client. Treatment was found to be superior to no treatment for a group of women with orgasmic dysfunction.

In the framework illustrated by Figure 1, one can see that a great deal more needs to be known about this approach to sex therapy, including further identification of the key procedures leading to behavior change, replication of controlled studies of short-term efficacy, controlled studies of maintenance, and further knowledge concerning the mode of treatment, level of therapist training required, and so on. Once more, despite widespread application and the replacement of nonspecific approaches by a well-delineated procedure, much remains to be done to develop the necessary body of knowledge that could lead to well-grounded implementation.

Some Conclusions

The process of generating, testing, and implementing new therapeutic procedures is not simple, and for the most part, as we have seen, there are no shortcuts. To the extent that knowledge is missing, application will be uncertain. Moreover, no final therapeutic answer to a particular condition will be discovered. New discoveries will be made, which will lead to new theoretical and therapeutic developments, which must then be tested against the old. Obviously we are describing a dynamic interactive system of knowledge acquisition. In this context the notion of a crucial outcome experiment is obviously incorrect. All experimental work must be considered in the light of all existing studies.

This situation may not be dissimilar to that of another intervention field—medicine. Recently Comroe (1978, p. 931) wrote:

My father, practicing internal medicine in the mid-1930's, had a few drugs (digitalis, insulin, arsphenamine, vaccines) that improved, cured, or prevented disease, and a few more (aspirin, morphine, barbital) that relieved symptoms of distress. Mainly he provided his patients with hope, encouragement, relief of suffering, and laxatives to keep their bowels open, and he recommended excision of foci of infection (mainly tonsils) and plenty of fruit juices (he had no faith in chicken soup). I, teaching in the mid-1930's, had few honest answers to student questions except "I don't know." It was then I realized what research was all about. Research meant that a physician did not have to say, year after year, "I can't cure you" to the vast majority of his patients. In short, research meant the end of a long static period in medicine—because every one of the great advances in modern medicine and surgery has come through research.

Now, in the 1970s, the field of psychotherapy is emerging from its prescientific phase, when support and encouragement were all that therapists could offer their clients, to a period when a variety of specific procedures are becoming available for clients with particular problems. And this change is due to the impact of research of the last twenty years. Of necessity, much time must often elapse before useful applications result from research. This should not be viewed with dismay. For premature application of what eventually turns out to be an ineffective procedure carries with it enormous social costs, not the least of which involves the payment of fees for ineffective and often somewhat dangerous procedures.

7

Implications and Recommendations for Service Delivery, Training, and Research

Service Delivery

The long and sometimes tortuous path of developing a new therapy leads naturally to the question, At what point should a new procedure be applied? And, perhaps just as important, when should an old procedure be abandoned in favor of a more effective and perhaps less expensive therapy?

Unfortunately, such decisions are not made logically. Fad, fashion, and what one was taught, as well as considerations of the marketplace, are strong determinants of the behavior of clinicians. Moreover, data on new therapies are often difficult to interpret and offer less-than-conclusive guidance. Perhaps research can never provide complete guidance to the clinician, who is presented with a unique set of circumstances by each client.

Faced with a new theory, evaluative research, and practice, clinicians tend to integrate the new theory and practice with the old. Thus, hybrids such as psychodynamic behavior therapy have begun to flourish. Unfortunately, the theoretical frameworks of behavior therapy and psychoanalytic therapy are so disparate that no sensible merging of the two is possible. One framework views behavior as being influenced largely by current environmental events, while the other uses a quasi-illness model in which behavior reflects inner and hidden conflicts. Behavior therapy involves a direct approach to the problem behavior, while psychoanalytic therapy involves an indirect approach. Such differences cannot be reconciled.

An attempt to clarify the confused situation was put forward by Lazarus (1971), who advocated the notion of "technical eclecticism," in which the therapist is free to use any technique, derived from any system, without subscribing to theoretical underpinnings that do not enjoy empirical support. This is a reasonable idea and is probably close to the way in which new therapeutic procedures are used by therapists of different persuasions.

More recently, Lazarus (1976) proposed a "multimodal behavior therapy" in which clinical problems are analyzed in terms of seven separate yet interactive modalities: behavior, affect, sensation, imagery, cognition, interpersonal behavior, and drugs. Therapy focuses on specific difficulties within each modality. Although both social learning and cognitive behavior modification approaches emphasize the critical importance of symbolic processes such as imagery and cognitions in therapeutic change, Lazarus suggested that multimodal therapy is more comprehensive and systematic in its modification of these processes. While attractive because it promises to free therapists from outmoded theory and practice, multimodal therapy runs the risk of becoming yet another monolithic therapeutic enterprise unless it leads to careful evaluative research.

In fact, there is no simple answer for the clinician, since, as we have seen, there is much that is not known. This section will, therefore, examine some of the implications of recent developments in behavior therapy for the clinician and for service delivery.

Assessment of Behavior Problems

Many, if not most, disorders of behavior have been approached as if they were medical or organic problems. While such an approach is useful when applied to disorders such as the psychoses, it is inappropriate when applied to other disorders, such as the neuroses or the so-called personality disorders, without sufficient regard for the need of a different conceptual approach. Thus, the notions of diagnosis and prognosis, applicable to physical disorders that progress logically from one phase of illness to another, are not appropriate for the majority of behavior disorders, which are so dependent for their form on unpredictable changes in the social environment.

Such disorders require an approach that recognizes the complexity and variability of behavior and its unique environmental determinants. Problem areas should be defined on an individual basis and with sufficient objectivity so that, at the very least, clients can monitor their own behavior. Preferably, of course, the clinician should also be able to measure some aspect of the problem by way of an observable behavior to ensure that behavior and not verbal report alone will change during the course of therapy. Moreover, the functional relationship between behavior and its environmental determinants needs to be ascertained as exactly as possible within the limits of the therapeutic situation.

As suggested earlier, the single-case experiment may be a useful clinical tool in analyzing therapeutic response to well-defined procedures and in determining the future course of therapy. Thus, particular aspects of a therapeutic program can be removed and then reinstated while observing the effect on ongoing behavior. Obviously, such a procedure cannot become routine clinical practice because of the technical difficulties involved, many of which were discussed earlier. Nonetheless, for difficult therapeutic problems, this method may provide valuable insights into the active components of therapy.

The Therapeutic Encounter

For the therapist faced with each client's unique problems, the findings of the experimental behavioral sciences concerning the specificity of therapeutic results are by no means reassuring, although such findings are compatible with the difficulties that therapists encounter in helping clients to change their behaviors. Problems such as limited generalization of improvement, insight without behavior change, and the need for clients to practice new behaviors within a favorable social environment are known to therapists of all persuasions.

Therapeutic interchanges encompass several components. One component can be conceptualized as a general helping relationship. Within this relationship, the behavior change variables so far identified include therapeutic instructions, modeling, and reinforcing transactions, as well as factors with less clear effects, such as the reformulation of problems and imparting advice. Also included within this class

of rather poorly specified therapeutic procedures are
the following, noted by Agras (1973, p. 169):

These skills include the ability to form a working relationship
with patients (clients, students), their families, the involved
community, and other therapeutic staff. Such a working relationship embraces characteristics to be found in helpful human
encounters, including the ability to offer hope for a solution to
problems, a rational context in which to understand problems,
and a rationale for change.... Clinician[s] must also be aware of
the total needs of the ... client and be able to fit [their] endeavors
into an overall program of care. This implies an awareness of the
variety of problem behaviors encountered in any given population and of the possible causes of such behavior, whether
psychologic or environmental, so that appropriate referral can be
made and adequate consultation obtained.

Equally important is the willingness to follow through with a
treatment program despite the uncertainties and vicissitudes
that beset therapists. Indeed, the ability to deal with ambiguous
and uncertain situations when one is operating within that vast
shadowy area of the partly known, and to carry through a
therapeutic program despite these hazards, is an essential
therapist characteristic.

Doubtless, as research into the therapeutic
encounter proceeds, the precise effect of many of the
variables described above will be delineated, as will
the exact procedures needed to achieve more
precisely defined ends. Nonspecific therapeutic factors will be identified and specified. Only then will
training in the establishment of a therapeutic relationship become reliable and measurable instead of
being left to chance and uncertainty, as is presently
the case.

Initiating Behavior Change

While a satisfactory therapeutic relationship seems to
be a prerequisite for clinical behavior change, it is not

enough.[1] To increase the effectiveness of therapy, specific behavior change procedures must be added. Thus, the behavior to be changed must be well defined, and an opportunity to practice the new behavior under favorable conditions must be afforded. This may require the construction of somewhat artificial therapeutic environments, for example, devising fear-provoking situations in which the phobic can practice regularly rather than being dependent on the infrequent and randomly occurring exposure that occurs in daily life. Procedures such as therapeutic instructions, prompting required behavior, modeling new behavior, reinforcement, and feedback of progress in changing behavior which implies monitoring of behavior change by the client or therapist, as well as the use of imaginal procedures, have all been shown to facilitate the acquisition of new behavior across a remarkably wide variety of problems. Indeed, one of the major contributions of behavior therapy during the past 20 years has been defining the specific procedures involved in facilitating behavior change and in experimentally demonstrating the short-term efficacy of such procedures.

Generalization and Maintenance

As we have also seen, however, such procedures, if applied only in the therapeutic setting, will show imperfect generalization to the client's environment. Thus, a new behavior must be practiced, either in settings that resemble the client's world or in the ac-

---

[1]This does not apply to self-help programs, such as bibliotherapy, where no therapist is involved. However, as we note elsewhere, such programs have not been adequately evaluated and may not be as effective as therapist-conducted programs.

tual environment. This may, for example, require the development of intermediate living and working arrangements to allow transfer of behavior from a hospital ward to the real world. Or it may require therapists to accompany patients to a variety of real-life settings or to enlist the aid of family members as auxiliary therapists to help with homework assignments, an increasingly used therapeutic strategy.

In addition, behavior change programs should be designed to increase the individual's independence and competence as rapidly as possible so that external control of behavior by the therapeutic regime can be reduced quickly and ultimately terminated. A considerable amount of laboratory research provides potential guidelines for facilitating diverse self-control efforts. After participants adopt new patterns of behavior, the next phase in the program may require direct training in self-reinforcement. This is achieved by gradually transferring evaluation of performance from the therapist to the client. Rewards can then be made contingent not only on the occurrence of desired behavior but also on accurate self-evaluation of performance.

Once accurate self-evaluative behavior is established, the reinforcing function is transferred from the therapist so that individuals now evaluate their own behaviors and reinforce themselves appropriately. Artificial material or social rewards are gradually reduced as the person's behavior is increasingly brought under the control of self-administered and symbolic consequences. The ultimate aim of training in self-reinforcement is to produce a level of functioning at which participants can control their own behaviors with a minimum of external constraints and artificial inducements (Bandura, 1969).

In practice, this transition may take time to achieve, and it often remains incomplete. This may be due to the relative paucity of research into the mechanisms underlying the generalization and maintenance of clinical behavior change. In addition, however, newly acquired social behavior is dependent on appropriate environmental support. Favorable amounts of positive feedback and reinforcement from others are essential to avoid extinction. Unfortunately, such reinforcement does not always exist and often cannot be instated in the client's world.

This, of course, brings us to a consideration of some of the limits of therapy. Therapeutic behavior change cannot occur in individuals who live in conditions in which the new behavior will not be reinforced or may not even be adaptive. In such cases, the environment requires changing. And while, as we will see in the next section, certain aspects of environmental change fall under the domain of psychology, others involve the remediation of major social problems for which no ready answer presently exists.

New Directions for Therapeutic Services

So far we have shown that therapy is becoming increasingly well specified as new therapeutic techniques proceed from hypothesis through laboratory demonstration and short- and long-term controlled therapeutic trials to application. Such increasing specificity is leading to a new trend toward the delivery of therapeutic services within specialty clinics, a phenomenon that is likely to become widespread during the next decade. Behavior problems (such as sexual and marital disorders), eating disorders (including obesity and anorexia nervosa), stress-related disorders (such as tension headache), and phobia and compulsive disorders—to mention only a few—are well-delineated problems that can be treated with relatively well-researched specific procedures. Since such disorders are often associated with particular secondary or complicating problems, for example, interpersonal problems in sexual disorders, quite complex programs can be devised to assess and treat both the primary and secondary problems. Ideally, such specialty clinics would carefully assess their results and engage in research to refine their therapeutic procedures. In this way, potentially cost-effective therapies should emerge.

Well-specified therapeutic procedures lead to the possibility that services can be provided by somewhat more narrowly trained personnel. There appears to be both a growing need for such persons (called paraprofessionals or, as O'Leary and Wilson [1975] suggested, psychological assistants) and a growing number of programs to train these people. Psychological assistants work as members of a therapeutic team and can carry out a number of well-specified procedures at least as well as their professional colleagues. The classroom has been one site where such persons have been demonstrated useful, as has the mental hospital and the halfway house. Moreover, as Marks and his colleagues have recently illustrated, specially trained nurses can use specific procedures as effectively as psychiatrists; moreover, they can bring therapeutic services to the housebound client.

It is our view that the training of such personnel should expand with the development of specific behavior change procedures. Whether such workers should be subject to certification and recertification procedures is at present an open question, since they do not always fit into an existing professional grouping. One future possibility is that a new professional —the behavior analyst—will emerge.

The model of therapy so far presented fits well with current methods of delivering therapeutic services, be they in a therapist's office, a mental hospital ward, a halfway house, or a classroom. Yet, throughout this book it has been suggested that an alternative view of the majority of behavior problems may be more productive. For the most part, individuals with such disorders either have unwanted troublesome behaviors or lack certain skills in living. What they need is an opportunity to learn new and more effective ways of behaving, a conceptualization congruent with an educational approach. Such an approach might have many advantages: Patients would become students and be given the opportunity to understand their own problems and to learn to change their own behavior.

Courses aimed at achieving specific behavior change might be offered both by educational and therapeutic institutions. Such courses would include information concerning the problem and an opportunity to acquire and practice new behavior, at first in the classroom and then in the student's environment, with a structured sequence of homework involving family members. Some examples of this approach already exist, such as courses in assertiveness training. At least one quite comprehensive program is in operation that offers a basic sequence in self-assessment, as well as several series of behavior change courses, having titles such as "Aging and Retirement Readiness," "Behavior Rehearsal Workshop," "Job Interview Skills," and "Relaxation Training."

While no formal evaluation of this program has yet
been completed, the sponsors consider that they
have reached a population that might otherwise have
gone untreated (Bakker and Armstrong, 1976).

To reach more people with well-specified problems, well-tested packaged programs need to be developed. Some packages already exist for weight control, toilet training, and enhancing assertiveness.
Such therapies are well specified and include manuals for both instructor and client and methods for
assessing the program's efficacy. Moreover, they are
often designed for application by therapists without a
doctoral degree, thus decreasing the expense of ad-
ministration. The number of well-tested packaged
therapies will undoubtedly increase during the next
decade, perhaps followed by the evolution of equally
well-tested self-management programs in which no
therapist will be required. However, we hypothesize
that as one moves from therapist-conducted indi-
vidualized therapy to packaged programs and to
self-help manuals, a distinct falloff in therapeutic effect will occur. This dropoff will be tolerable, at least
for some behavior problems, provided that it is bal-
anced by increased cost-effectiveness.

As we have seen, many behavior problems are
strongly influenced by the individual's personal
environment, and at times such environmental
influences will impede individuals' attempts to alter
their behaviors. In such cases, an approach to the
entire environment may be required. Such social
engineering may be seen in primitive form in the use
of highly contrived token economy systems in the
school, hospital ward, or family. Obviously there is
much to learn about this approach; nonetheless, a
small but growing experimental literature, aimed at a
variety of community problems, already exists and

may be the precursor of an important new development in therapeutic behavior change.

Such attempts to change the social and physical environment to enhance behavior change and thus the individual's capacity to live more fully bring us to the topic of prevention—not only of problems in living but also of physical illness. For it is clear from epidemiologic research that behaviors such as overeating, too little exercise, and cigarette smoking are associated with both cardiovascular disease and some forms of cancer. The remedy lies with individuals themselves, providing that health becomes the concern of everyone rather than what Kristein, Arnold, and Wynder (1977) termed a disease-oriented medical care system.

As Somers (1977, p. 962) pointed out:

1. Responsibility for personal health rests primarily with the individual: not with government, not with physicians or hospitals, not with any third-party financial program. Meaningful national health policies must be directed to increasing, rather than eroding, the individual's sense of responsibility for his own health and his ability to understand and cope with health problems.

2. If the individual's responsibility is to be effectively discharged, it must be supported by social policies designed to provide him with essential environmental protection, health information, and access to health care when needed.

With all this we agree; however, as we have seen, more is needed to achieve these ends. It is essential to provide an opportunity for individuals to acquire the necessary skills to lead healthier lives, and it is the task of a scientifically oriented applied psychology to lay the foundation for the services required to meet this goal.

One example of a successful community-wide behavior change effort points the way to the future. A media campaign, extending over a three-year period, was directed toward smoking cessation, dietary change and weight loss, and increased exercise. This campaign was found to lower the risk of cardiovascular disease in the treated community. Moreover, a combination of skills training offered in a group setting during the media campaign much enhanced the degree of behavior change.

Similar educational behavior change efforts might be used in a variety of circumstances. Some of the principles of information dissemination and contingency management seem to have been used successfully in response to the recent severe drought in California. The combination of information, appeal, and contingencies led to substantial water conservation by most of the affected population.

Thus behavior therapy (no longer a very appropriate term) has gone well beyond providing services within the traditional client-therapist relationship. Such developments will comprise some of the most interesting aspects of behavior therapy in the next 20 years, hopefully bringing the benefits of advances in our understanding of human behavior to the many who are neglected by the present structure of therapeutic services.

Training

While there are many categories of behavior change agents, referred to here as therapists for convenience, we will concentrate on the implications of what we have discussed for training in two professions— psychology and psychiatry. The developments in theory, research method, and specific therapeutic approaches pose challenges to both fields.

Training in Clinical Psychology

As Azrin (1977) suggested, doctoral training in applied psychology, which has grown out of university-based academic departments of psychology, tends to sidetrack both the potential clinician and the applied research worker. Too often such programs have a weak applied focus and are taught by faculty with inadequate clinical experience and little clinical responsibility. This is in part a consequence of the emergence of clinical psychology from within academic departments on campuses that offer students little opportunity to become involved with anything but the most transient behavior problems in limited populations, such as those found in student counseling centers.

If the clinical training is not broad enough, research training is also too narrow for a field that must be concerned with both the process and outcome of human behavior change. Azrin (1977) suggested that the academic requirements of psychology too often immerse the beginning researcher in the formal aspects of research and encourage "simple noncontroversial response measures that belie the unpredictability of outcome" (p. 142) rather than the tackling of important social problems and consideration of both process and outcome, including follow-up to ascertain the stability of achieved change.

Psychology training centers should offer supervised experience with a variety of behavior problems in several service settings. Within each of these settings, psychology faculty should have adequate control of the client population with, of course, responsibility for the population. Such faculty would consist of academic clinicians, whose range of functions and responsibilities would be similar to that of a present-day medical school faculty. Such training centers would also be expected to experiment with service delivery systems, such as those taking an educational approach to behavior problems, as discussed in the previous section.

The developing trend in clinical psychology training toward the professional school would seem to fit nicely with developments in behavior therapy. Such schools should, however, be part of a university, be located in an area large enough to afford a suitable clinical population, and reflect the relationship between the clinic and science by being closely tied to an academic department of psychology. The faculty should be capable of teaching applied psychology, and the school should offer appropriate courses in related behavioral and biological sciences that are directed to the future clinician and applied researcher. Active programs of applied research should be pursued by the faculty of such schools, as should relevant basic research, thus achieving the vigorous reciprocal interaction between the applied and basic sciences that should be a hallmark of this experimental clinical endeavor. Professional schools of psychology without this close relationship will tend to drift into the dogmatic teaching of therapeutic skills, a tendency already too frequent in the clinic. The majority of students within the professional school will become clinicians. However, a substantial minority should become clinical researchers, and the curriculum should be flexible enough to train both types of professionals.

Training in Psychiatry and Medicine

The notion that behavior therapy represents a new theoretical, methodologial, and therapeutic approach to disorders of human behavior has implications for both medical and psychiatric education. First and foremost, the findings and applications of this field should be taught not only to psychiatric residents but also to medical students at an appropriate level.

This need for an increased emphasis on the science of human behavior has already been recognized by the inclusion of a considerable number of courses in the behavioral sciences within the medical school curriculum and by the increasing number of psychologists to be found within the medical school setting. But even these developments are not without their problems. The typical course in the behavioral sciences within medical schools tends to be weighted toward the descriptive sciences, is often heavily biologically oriented, and does not focus on application. Moreover, even though the number of psychologists both in medical schools and in departments of psychiatry is growing, in a recent survey 43 percent of all psychiatric residency programs reported only rudimentary interdisciplinary collaboration in training (Gurel, 1973). The same survey revealed that only 36 percent of psychiatric residency programs offered experience in behavior therapy, while 100 percent offered training in the procedures of individual psychoanalytically oriented psychotherapy.

These are disappointing findings, for surely psychiatry as a medical discipline should be based on a scientific approach to human behavior, and there is no doubt that the expansion of knowledge in this area is comparable to that in the field of psychopharmacology. What is needed now is the development of an applied medical psychology that will bring to the attention of physicians, and particularly to residents in psychiatry, the growing variety of specific procedures that derive from psychology.

Applied psychology, like physiology, might be taught by either Ph.D.s or M.D.s, providing, of course, that the physician is an expert in the subject matter. In our view, it will be necessary to train a cadre of psychiatrist behavioral scientists who are capable of teaching and conducting research in this branch of experimental therapeutics and who might lead the way toward cooperative clinical research between the behavioral and biological sciences.

Behavioral Medicine—A New Model?

A suitable format for some of these developments may now be emerging in the form of behavioral medicine, a new area whose growth has been catalyzed by behavior therapy. At a recent conference (Schwartz and Weiss, 1977, p. 4), behavioral medicine was defined as "the field concerned with the development of behavioral science knowledge and techniques relevant to the understanding of physical health and illness, and the application of this knowledge and techniques to prevention, diagnosis, treatment, and rehabilitation." The interdisciplinary nature of the field was recognized with contributions from disciplines such as psychology, sociology, anthropology, education, epidemiology, biostatistics, psychiatry, and medicine.

This development recognizes that environmental factors in the broadest sense contribute to much of the disease and disability suffered by humanity today. The findings of epidemiology and the descriptive behavioral sciences form the basis from which the intervention-oriented behavioral sciences can proceed. The next wave of advances in preventive medicine may derive from this new combination as more effective approaches to problems such as obesity, too little exercise, poor diet, excessive alcohol consumption, and cigarette smoking are developed. A promising area is the research on essential hypertension. Epidemiologic work has identified social and environmental factors that contribute to the etiology of the disorder. Basic psychological research has examined the role of environmental stressors in inducing the disorder and factors involved in the pathogenesis of high blood pressure in animals. At the same time, interest has focused on the use of relaxation therapy and blood pressure feedback in the treatment of essential hypertension and on the problem of and remediation of poor adherence to the medical regimen.

This type of interdisciplinary development offers new challenges for the training of professionals from a wide variety of backgrounds in the experimental and therapeutic procedures involved in behavioral medicine. Such programs are likely to be located in medical settings, which have a favorable environment for interdisciplinary collaboration, and will result in the training of clinician scientists with new sets of skills who might work in a variety of medical or community settings.

Continuing Education

The clinician will need to keep abreast of the growing array of specific behavior change techniques and the anticipated trend toward increasingly specific procedures. Moreover, as is the case in medicine, practitioners will need to be aware of developments in basic science in order to bring the most sophisticated viewpoint to their clients' behavior problems. No longer can a trained psychotherapist practice in the same way during an entire career. As specific procedures are added to the basic client-therapist relationship, the need for therapists to change their ways, both in psychology and psychiatry, will become increasingly evident. Thus, in the professional school of psychology as well as in medical schools, continuing education departments should offer opportunities for therapists to acquire new information and to learn new skills.

Unfortunately this is often no easy task. New behavior change procedures can be complex, and therapists will need to learn theory, assessment procedures, therapeutic skills, and perhaps evaluation methods. In practice, the most convenient way to achieve this end may be for the practitioner to form a fairly permanent relationship with an institution offering such programs, so that a continuing and sensible course of instruction can be offered. Doubtless, such continuing education will become mandated in both professions, perhaps in the form of periodic recertification. Such procedures should be actively encouraged by the professions and hopefully, enthusiastically embraced by practitioners who wish to provide the best possible service to their clients.

Research

As we consider the implications for research of the data and arguments reviewed and presented in this volume, many issues already considered in some detail will reappear. As we saw in Chapter 6, the progression of therapy research may follow different patterns for different problems or procedures. Yet, in each case that we examined, progress toward application was held up or made less certain because some aspects of research had not been given adequate attention. Investigators and funding agencies must develop the studies necessary to ensure smooth progress from the generation of a new therapeutic procedure to its eventual application. An overconcentration of studies at one particular stage of development should be avoided, since it gives rise to a sense of futility, of missing the proverbial forest for the trees.

The traditional therapeutic outcome experiment, for so long regarded as the hallmark of psychotherapy research, should be abandoned. The use of inappropriate outcome measures and inadequate specification of therapeutic procedures is largely responsible for the poor returns obtained from the demanding comparative studies of different therapies. All too often the results have been ambiguous or obscured. Certainly the limited conclusions one can draw from them do not justify the effort expended. A new measurement technology has been developed during the past 20 years that should supplant the old. Direct behavioral measures, psychophysiological measures, and self-report based on self-monitoring of well-specified behaviors are now available for many common behavior problems, and new measures are being developed. Future comparative studies must use such specific measures carried out, when possible, in the clients' natural environment. Moreover, the full range of experimental methods described in Chapters 4 and 5 should be used to develop the complex knowledge base needed for implementing a new, well-specified therapy.

In particular, we would argue for the funding of

programs of research centered around a particular problem or procedure, in which a series of related experiments would test a set of hypotheses. Such series of experiments would proceed logically through the phase of testing as outlined in Figure 1 to eventual application. This research should evaluate the long-term outcome of behavior change procedures, although we realize that many factors militate against such follow-up. If nothing else, follow-up is costly in time, effort, and money. The average clinical Ph.D. is completed in four or five years. In the normal course of affairs, the student must work up a line of research, develop an idea for a doctoral dissertation, carry out preliminary work in collecting pilot data, implement and complete the study, and finally write the dissertation. It is difficult, if not impossible, for a long-term follow-up to be conducted by the student with such time constraints.

New assistant professors are frequently preoccupied with completing sufficient research so that they can be promoted and eventually receive tenure. These reinforcement contingencies dictate research studies that are likely to be completed successfully, i.e., statistically significant results that permit publication in prestigious journals. The greater the number of publications, the greater the probability of promotion and tenure. A long-term follow-up investigation with its time demands, uncertainty of outcome, and delay in obtaining publishable data is, in many departments, a high-risk activity that discourages the most committed of clinical researchers.

Thus, a program devoted to long-term research, headed by a senior investigator free from these pressures, who directs junior colleagues in completing time-limited work, would be an effective way of supporting such clinical research. In turn, this may mean changes in the funding mechanisms to ensure the length of support necessary to evaluate these longer-term issues. In any event, the field has advanced to the point where these issues require urgent attention.

High priority should be given to studying the problem of generalization of therapeutic effects, identifying procedures to promote generalization from one situation to another, and maintaining behavior change over time. Much progress has been made in achieving acute behavior change, but most studies have either paid inadequate attention to the problems of generalization and maintenance or have demonstrated the existence of problems in these areas. We know too little about the factors involved in long-term maintenance of behavior, particularly in free-living populations not amenable to the constant supervision available in institutional settings. Both basic and applied studies in this important area are sorely needed.

Of course, research should be continued that has already demonstrated some effectiveness in children's behavior problems, phobias and compulsive behavior, long-term psychoses, mental retardation, and alcoholism. However, several promising and relatively new areas merit support and attention at this time. Among these are applications of behavior therapy to medical problems, the area referred to previously as behavioral medicine. Interesting and promising work has emerged in the treatment of chronic pain, cardiovascular problems, obesity, hypertension, and certain cardiac arrhythmias and in helping patients adhere to medical regimes. Most of this work, as is proper in a developing field, has examined only immediate behavior change, and studies aimed at understanding the process of behavior change in this interesting new area have barely begun. Another emergent area is the combination of psychopharmacological approaches and behavior therapy. Problems where such combinations may prove more effective than either treatment alone include phobia, depression, and obesity.

Other areas of promise involve prevention. Here two problems seem of immediate relevance—preventing the onset of crippling fears and phobias and reducing cardiovascular risk by behavior change procedures. These areas, since they involve approaches to entire communities, are linked with a final area of promise, community applications of behavior change techniques. Intriguing work on problems such as fuel conservation, littering, and even aspects of community organization has been published within the last five years. Such work, which may provide some solutions to pressing social problems, deserves encouragement. Clearly, directing therapeutic efforts at individuals is much more expensive than employing preventive measures and community behavior change.

Related to the community approach is the development of alternatives to the usual therapist-client relationship. Many services can be provided within an educational context in order to bring much needed help to a larger number of persons than is possible within a therapist-intensive system. Demonstration projects with built-in evaluations of efficacy would seem to be an appropriate approach to this particular issue.

Another related concern is the accurate assessment of the needs for various forms of services in communities and methods to determine the relative priorities for service delivery. Obviously, such concerns will lead to determination of the social costs and benefits of behavior therapy, again emphasizing the need for assessment of long-term outcome and for adequate measurement systems. Finally, behavior therapy is an applied field that can only flourish with strong basic research in psychology. Such support should continue with every encouragement to foster wherever possible a fruitful interaction between basic and applied research workers.

8
Summary and Overview

Although still controversial in some quarters, behavior therapy is now a flourishing part of the therapeutic establishment. Its influence on the practice of psychological treatment methods has been considerable and its impact has changed the face of research on therapeutic process and outcome.

Behavior therapy is a constantly evolving approach to the assessment and treatment of behavior disorders and has changed significantly during the past two decades. In contrast to its earlier conceptualization of applying conditioning principles to emotional disorders, behavior therapy today is both more complex and more sophisticated. Instead of a monolithic approach, there is a diversity of views encompassing different research strategies and a broad range of heterogeneous treatment techniques with different rationales; there is also open debate about theoretical issues, methodological requirements and evidence of efficacy. Among the distinctive emphases that can be identified within contemporary behavior therapy are applied behavior analysis, a neo-behavioristic S-R model, social learning theory, cognitive behavior modification, and multimodal behavior therapy.

Despite this catholicity of views, two common characteristics of behavior therapy emerge: the acceptance of a psychological model of human behavior that differs from the conventional psychodynamic, or quasi-disease, model of mental illness; and a commitment to scientific method, measurement, and evaluation. In terms of the former, many types of abnormal behavior that are regarded as illnesses or signs of illness are interpreted as non-pathological problems of living best treated directly with behavioral methods. The emphasis is on the current determinants of behavior, and specificity is the hallmark of assessment, treatment, and evaluation strategies. In terms of the latter characteristic, behavior therapy prizes replicable and testable methods that are consistent with experimental-clinical psychology.

Behavior therapy is behavioristic only in the methodological sense, and private events or cognitive processes are emphasized in most current approaches. Contrary to some stereotypes, behavior therapy is neither mechanistic and impersonal nor superficial and symptomatic treatment. The therapist-client relationship is an integral part of the clinical practice of behavior therapy, and treatment is designed to address *all* the factors that are causing or maintaining the client's problems. Behavior therapy differs from traditional psychodynamic approaches not in denying the importance of the causes of psychological disorders but in identifying their nature. Finally, behavior therapists have been active in clarifying the importance of ethical issues in therapeutic change and have developed specific recommendations concerning the ethical practice of therapy.

Behavior therapy has stimulated much research with a variety of disorders. Although the amount and quality of evidence varies across disorders, much can be said about the efficacy of treatment in given areas. Within the neurotic disorders, major advances have been made in identifying effective treatments for anxiety and phobic reactions. These techniques include systematic desensitization, flooding, participant modeling, and reinforced practice. Obsessive-compulsive disorders have received less research attention, but procedures such as flooding and response prevention have been shown to be effective here as well.

Sexual dysfunction and disorders have been treated with diverse procedures. The most outstanding developments have been made in the treatment of sexual dysfunction by using the procedures developed by Masters and Johnson. Yet other approaches based more on reinforcement procedures have altered disorders such as transsexualism, exhibitionism, and fetishism.

Behavioral treatment of marital discord has received relatively little outcome research, at least with severely disturbed marriages. Preliminary work has suggested that marriages can be improved with training in interaction and communication skills. Incentive approaches, often conducted by the spouses directly in the home, have been demonstrated to be effective in selected reports.

Addictive behaviors such as alcoholism, cigarette smoking, and drug use encompass a large number of treatments. Excessive alcohol consumption has been treated primarily with aversion therapy and incentive programs. Cigarette smoking has been treated effectively with self-control procedures and an aversion technique referred to as rapid smoking. Drug use has received much less attention.

Psychotic disorders include many forms of deviant behavior that have been effectively altered. Treatment techniques, based primarily on operant conditioning, have decreased psychotic and aggressive behaviors and have increased social interaction and communication. The results of programs that focus on specific behaviors show improvement in the discharge and readmission rates of hospitalized patients.

A wide range of childhood disorders, varying in degrees of severity, have been treated. Incentive programs have been applied to hyperactivity, autism, delinquency, and self-stimulation with some success. With the mentally retarded similar incentive programs have altered a variety of behaviors, including self-care, social, language, and community skills.

Behavioral treatments have been applied to many medical and psychophysiological disorders. Relaxation, biofeedback, and incentive techniques have altered such disorders as hypertension, insomnia, anorexia nervosa, and a host of others. Applications with the aged, mostly based on operant techniques, have altered self-care and social interaction. In education, an area outside the traditional scope of mental health, behavioral techniques have been employed to accelerate academic performance and improve deportment in students ranging from preschool to college levels. Community extensions of behavior modification have focused on socially relevant concerns such as job finding, pollution control, and energy conservation. Applications of behavioral techniques to medicine, the aged, and community problems are relatively recent developments. Even so, considerable research has established the impact of select behavioral techniques.

Overall, the striking feature of behavior therapy

at the present stage of development is the remarkable breadth of applications. The evidence is not uniformly convincing or sophisticated in all instances. Yet considerable advances have been made in concrete areas where a number of techniques exist, and more effective treatments can be distinguished. Many, indeed perhaps most, areas covered have shown considerable promise with a continuing acceleration of research.

Turning to the question of the comparative efficacy of various psychotherapeutic approaches, we find that conventional comparative clinical outcome research has been directed toward answering two questions: Is psychotherapy superior to no treatment? Is one form of therapy superior to another? Such studies have invariably evaluated the effects of ill-defined treatment approaches on heterogeneous problems using global outcome measures. As a result of numerous conceptual and methodological inadequacies, the majority of these studies are largely uninterpretable.

Despite the serious methodological shortcomings of the research, conclusions of far-reaching significance continue to be drawn. Thus recent reviews of comparative outcome studies have alleged that psychotherapy is superior to no treatment and that alternative psychological treatment methods do not differ significantly in their effects. These conclusions have been criticized as premature in an evaluation of conventional outcome research by Kazdin and Wilson (1978).

Conventional outcome research has resulted in studies in which potential treatment differences are inevitably obscured. It follows that the practice of conducted box-score analyses or meta-analyses, in which aggregate sets of different outcome studies are contrasted, simply compounds the existing ambiguity. Among other serious failings, these between-study evaluations ignore the methodological quality of individual studies, treat different outcome measures as functionally equivalent, give equal weight to studies of varying sophistication and quality, and set up a form of majority rule in which several poorly designed studies are accorded more importance than a single well-controlled one.

Traditional psychotherapy research has been restricted largely to global outcome measures and has also been limited in the breadth of criteria used to evaluate treatment. More specific and more varied outcome measures need to be used, including assessment of the importance of the therapeutic change, the side effects of treatment, the durability of treatment effects, cost-effectiveness of treatment, the efficiency of treatment, and the acceptability of the treatment procedures and goals to potential consumers.

Aside from greater specificity and expansion of treatment criteria, evaluation of therapy can be enhanced by using well-controlled laboratory settings to evaluate treatment. This research, often considered to be an analogue of the clinical situation, has permitted careful evaluation and development of treatment packages and examination of components necessary and sufficient for therapeutic change. Concerns have been voiced that the conditions of laboratory research, such as the focus on relatively mild target problems in college students, may limit the generality of findings. Yet, laboratory research, only one facet of the evaluation of any treatment, has helped answer questions that could not be posed in a clinical situation. Whether the results can be extended to clinical treatment is an empirical matter to be evaluated in its own right.

Clinical situations often are not amenable to experimental evaluation of treatment. One reason for this is the absence of a large homogeneous group of clients. Yet the clinic provides an opportunity to evaluate treatment in a single-case experiment. These experiments require continuous assessment of behavior over time and specific designs to evaluate treatment. Although these conditions cannot always be met, single-case experiments have provided dramatic demonstrations of the efficacy of behavioral treatment with a range of severe clinical problems.

Evaluation of therapy encompasses several different research strategies and questions about treatment. These strategies as a whole ask questions pertaining to the following: the overall treatment package, components that may be added to enhance treatment, necessary and sufficient ingredients to effect therapeutic change, parameters that can be varied to maximize efficacy, comparisons with other treatments, client and therapist variables that contribute to treatment, and the processes of therapeutic change during the course of treatment.

In addition to the use of a broader range of research strategies, clinical research needs to progress through a series of stages, each of which may alter the current status of the intervention field. Basic research, theoretical considerations, and clinical observation, together with uncontrolled tests in a clinical population, lead to the development of new intervention procedures. Such procedures should then be subject to short-term evaluation, along with laboratory, analogue, and clinical studies to illuminate therapeutic mechanisms. Following this, studies should be aimed at evaluating and enhancing the generalization and maintenance of treatment effects and the components and parameters of treatment. Only then should longer-term evaluation of the efficacy of treatment be carried out, together with comparative outcome studies.

An evaluation of a number of research areas in behavior therapy reveals some progress through this chain of research. However, longer-term assessment of efficacy and studies considering issues of maintenance and generalization are sorely needed in most of the areas examined.

The present-day development of behavior therapy and the research issues examined naturally lead to a series of recommendations concerning therapy, training, and research. These recommendations are summarized below.

Assessment

• Broad diagnostic categories should be replaced by problem identification characterized by specific objective and subjective measures, which should be quantifiable and, where possible, observable by the client who can then monitor progress.

Therapy

• Specific behavior change procedures should be added to the (as yet) relatively poorly defined client-therapist relationship. The process of therapy should include procedures to effect initial behavior change, to reinforce that change, and to ensure generalization and maintenance.

• Specialized clinics or centers, capable of treating both a specific primary problem and associated problems, should be encouraged, particularly when there is sufficient evidence to demonstrate the effectiveness of a particular procedure in a given problem area. Promising areas for such specialized services include phobia, compulsive disorders, eating disorders, sexual problems, the oppositional child, and perhaps such disorders as insomnia and tension headache.

• The level of therapist best suited for widespread delivery of particular therapeutic services should be empirically determined. Many services can be provided by psychological assistants or nurses who have been specifically trained.

• Many services would best be delivered within an educational format rather than as a traditional mental health service. Common problems in living (often characterized as personality disorders) might best be helped by teaching specific interpersonal skills to enhance personal functioning.

• In addition, a community-oriented approach might be appropriate for the solution of more widespread problems. Aspects of community functioning, such as fuel conservation, maintaining an attractive environment, and enhancing a healthy life-style, are examples of problems where such an approach might be useful.

Training

• Training in clinical psychology should aim at producing both skilled clinicians and a smaller number of clinician researchers. Training institutions should have control over and access to a variety of clinical settings and populations, should foster a healthy interaction between basic and applied sciences, and should be involved in the planning and execution of innovative service delivery.

• The teaching of applied behavioral science in schools of medicine should be fostered. Residency training programs in psychiatry should devote at least as much attention to the teaching of specific behavior change techniques as they presently provide for the poorly specified psychotherapies. Departments of psychiatry should foster research inquiry into both basic and applied aspects of behavior therapy.

• The development of behavioral medicine as an effective area of interdisciplinary enquiry should be fostered.

• Continuing education programs for both clinical psychology and psychiatry should provide the necessary knowledge base concerning the effectiveness of specific behavior change strategies. Opportunities for clinicians to acquire new therapeutic skills should also be provided.

Research

• The traditional psychotherapy outcome study characterized by poorly defined procedures and global measures of outcome should be abandoned.

• Funding agencies should promote research in overlooked areas such as the mechanisms of, and procedures needed to ensure, adequate generalization and maintenance of therapeutic effects.

• This, in turn, will require the funding of longer-term research and programs of research that will facilitate the research progression outlined in Figure 1.

• Specific content areas that should receive priority attention include the development of objective measures, applications to medical problems, community applications, and prevention.

References

Agras, W. S. Toward the certification of behavior therapists? *Journal of Applied Behavior Analysis*, *6*: 167 – 171, 1973.

Agras, W. S., Leitenberg, H., and Barlow O. H. Social reinforcement in the modification of agorophobia. *Archives of General Psychiatry*, *19*: 423 – 429, 1968.

Agras, W. S., et al. Behavior modification of anorexia nervosa. *Archives of General Psychiatry*, *30*: 279 – 286, 1974.

Agras, W. S., et al. *Behavior therapy: An evaluation.* Unpublished manuscript, Center for Advanced Study in the Behavioral Sciences, Stanford, Calif., July 1977.

Ayllon, T., Layman, D., and Kandel, H. J. A behavioral-educational alternative to drug control of hyperactive children. *Journal of Applied Behavior Analysis*, *8*: 137 – 146, 1975.

Azrin, N. H. A strategy for applied research: Learning based but outcome oriented. *American Psychologist*, *32*: 140 – 149, 1977.

Azrin, N. H. and Foxx, R. M. *Toilet training in less than a day.* New York: Simon & Schuster, 1974.

Azrin, B. H., et. al. Ethical issues for human services. *Behavior Therapy, 8,* 5 – 6, 1977.

Bachrach, A. J., Erwin, W. J., and Mohr, J. P. The control of eating behavior in an anorexic by operant conditioning techniques. In L. P. Ullmann and L. Krasner (eds.), *Case studies in behavior modification.* New York: Holt, Rinehart and Winston, 1965.

Baer, D. M., Wolf, M. M., and Risley, T. R. Some current dimensions of applied behavior analysis. *Journal of Applied Behavior Analysis, 1:* 91 – 97, 1968.

Bakker, C. B., and Armstrong, H. E. An educational approach to the delivery of mental health services. Unpublished manuscript, Adult Development Program, University of Washington, Seattle, 1976.

Bandura, A. *Principles of behavior modification.* New York: Holt, Rinehart and Winston, 1969.

Bandura, A. Self-efficacy: Toward a unifying theory of behavioral change. *Psychological Review, 84:* 191 – 215, 1977a.

Bandura, A. *Social learning theory.* Englewood Cliffs, N.J.: Prentice-Hall, 1977b.

Bandura, A., Blanchard, E. B., and Ritter, B. Relative efficacy of desensitization and modeling approaches for inducing behavioral, affective, and attitudinal changes. *Journal of Personality and Social Psychology, 5:* 16 – 22, 1967.

Beck, A. T. *Cognitive therapy and the emotional disorders.* New York: International Universities Press, 1976.

Boring, E. G. *A history of experimental psychology.* New York: Appleton-Century-Crofts, 1950.

Bornstein, M. R., Bellack, A. S., and Hersen, M. Social-skills training for unassertive children: A multiple-baseline analysis. *Journal of Applied Behavior Analysis, 10:* 183 – 195, 1977.

Ciminero, A. R. Behavioral assessment: An overview. In A. R. Ciminero, K. S. Calhoun, and H. E. Adams (eds.), *Handbook of behavioral assessment.* New York: Wiley, 1977.

Ciminero, A. R., Calhoun, K. S., and Adams, H. E. (eds.), *Handbook of behavioral assessment.* New York: Wiley, 1977.

Comroe, J. H. The road from research to new diagnosis and therapy. *Science, 200:* 931 – 937, 1978.

Davidson, G. C., and Stuart, R. B. Behavior therapy and civil liberties. *American Psychologist, 30:* 755 – 763, 1975.

Ellis, A. *The essence of rational psychotherapy: A comprehensive approach to treatment.* New York: Institute for Rational Living, 1970.

Eysenck, H. J. Learning theory and behaviour therapy. *Journal of Mental Science, 195:* 61 – 75, 1959.

Eysenck, H. J. The learning theory model of neurosis—a new approach. *Behaviour Research and Therapy, 14:* 251 – 268, 1976.

Farquhar, J. W., et al. Community education for cardiovascular health. *Lancet, 1:* 1192 – 1195, 1977.

Ferster, C. B., Nurnberger, J. I., and Levitt, E. B. The control of eating. *Journal of Mathematics, 1:* 87 – 109, 1962.

Fisher, S., and Greenberg, R. P. *The scientific credibility of Freud's theories and therapy.* New York: Basic Books, 1977.

Foa, E. B., and Goldstein, A. Prolonged exposure and strict response prevention in the treatment of obsessive-compulsive neurosis. *Behavior Therapy*, in press.

Fordyce, W. E., et al. Operant conditioning in the treatment of chronic pain. *Archives of Physical Medicine and Rehabilitation*, 54: 399 – 408, 1973.

Foxx, R. M., and Azrin, N. H. *Toilet training the retarded: A rapid program for day and night time independent toileting.* Champaign, Illinois: Research Press, 1973.

Franks, C. M., and Wilson, G. T. *Annual review of behavior therapy: Theory and practice*, vols. 1 – 6. New York: Brunner/Mazel, 1973 – 1978.

Gelder, M. G., et al. Specific and nonspecific factors in behavior therapy. *British Journal of Psychiatry*, 123: 445 – 462, 1973.

Goldiamond, J. Toward a constructional approach to social problems. *Behaviorism*, 2: 1 – 84, 1974.

Gurel, L. *A survey of academic resources in psychiatric training.* Washington, D.C.: American Psychiatric Association, 1973.

Hersen, M., and Barlow, D. H. *Single case experimental designs: Strategies for studying behavior change.* New York: Pergamon, 1976.

Jacob, R. G., Kraemer, H. C., and Agras, W. S. Relaxation therapy in the treatment of hypertension—a review. *Archives of General Psychiatry, 34:* 1417 – 1427, 1977.

Kazdin, A. E. *History of behavior modification.* Baltimore: University Park Press, 1978.

Kazdin, A. E. *Research design in clinical psychology.* New York: Harper & Row, 1979.

Kazdin, A. E., and Wilcoxon, L. A. Systematic desensitization and nonspecific treatment effects: A methodological evaluation. *Psychological Bulletin, 83:* 729 – 758, 1976.

Kazdin, A. E., and Wilson, G. T. *Evaluation of behavior therapy: Issues, evidence, and research strategies.* Cambridge, Mass.: Ballinger, 1978.

Keeley, S. M., Shember, K. M., and Carbonell, J. Operant clinical intervention: Behavior management or beyond? Where are the data? *Behavior Therapy, 7:* 292 – 305, 1976.

Kristein, M. S., Arnold, C. B., and Wynder, E. I. Health economics and preventive care. *Science, 195:* 457 – 462, 1977.

Lazarus, A. A. New methods in psychotherapy: A case study. *South African Medical Journal, 32:* 660 – 664, 1958.

Lazarus, A. A. Group therapy of phobic disorders by systematic desensitization. *Journal of Abnormal and Social Psychology, 63:* 504 – 510, 1961.

Lazarus, A. A. *Behavior therapy and beyond.* New York: McGraw-Hill, 1971.

Lazarus, A. A. *Multimodal behavior therapy.* New York: Springer, 1976.

Lazovik, A. D., and Lang, P. J. A laboratory demonstration of systematic desensitization psychotherapy. *Journal of Psychological Studies, 11:* 238 – 247, 1960.

Leitenberg, H. Behavioral approaches to treatment of neuroses. In H. Leitenberg (ed.), *Handbook of behavior modification and behavior therapy.* Englewood Cliffs, N.J.: Prentice-Hall, 1976.

Luborsky, L., Singer, B., and Luborsky, L. Comparative studies of psychotherapies: Is it true that everyone has won and all must have prizes? *Archives of General Psychiatry, 32:* 995 – 1008, 1975.

Mahoney, M. J. *Cognition and behavior modification.* Cambridge, Massachusetts: Ballinger, 1974.

Marks, I. M. Exposure: Clinical applications. In W. S. Agras (ed.), *Behavior modification: Principles and clinical applications.* Boston: Little-Brown, 1978.

Marks, I. M., et al. *Nursing in behavioral psychotherapy: An advanced clinical role for nurses.* London: Royal College of Nursing, 1977.

Marks, I. M., Hodgson, R., and Rachman, S. Treatment of chronic obsessive-compulsive neurosis by in-vivo exposure. *British Journal of Psychiatry, 127:* 349 – 464, 1975.

Masters, W. M., and Johnson, V. E. *Human sexual inadequacy.* Boston: Little, Brown, 1970.

Meichenbaum, D. *Cognitive behavior modification.* New York: Plenum Press, 1977.

Meyer, V., Levy, R., and Schnurer, A. The behavioral treatment of obsessive-compulsive disorders. In

H. R. Beech (ed.), *Obsessional states*. London: Methuen, 1974.

Mills, H., et al. Compulsive rituals treated by response prevention. *Archives of General Psychiatry, 28:* 524 — 529, 1973.

Mischel, W. Toward a cognitive social learning reconceptualization of personality. *Psychological Review, 80:* 252 — 283, 1973.

Nietzel, M. T., et al. *Behavioral approaches to community psychology.* New York: Pergamon, 1977.

O'Leary, K. D., and Wilson, G. T. *Behavior therapy: Application outcome.* Englewood Cliffs, N.J.: Prentice-Hall, 1975.

Paul, G. L. Outcome of systematic desensitization II: Controlled investigations of individual treatment, technique variations, and current status. In C. M. Franks (ed.), *Behavior therapy: Appraisal and status.* New York: McGraw-Hill, 1969.

Paul, G. L., and Lentz, R. J. *Psychosocial treatment of chronic mental patients: Milieu versus social-learning programs.* Cambridge, Mass.: Harvard University Press, 1977.

Peterson, D. R. *The clinical study of social behavior.* New York: Appleton-Century-Crofts, 1968.

Rachman, S. The conditioning theory of fear-acquisition: A critical examination. *Behaviour Research and Therapy, 15:* 375 — 388, 1977.

Rachman, S., and Hodgson, R. *Obsessions and compulsions.* Englewood Cliffs, N.J.: Prentice-Hall, 1978.

Schachter, S. Obesity and eating. *Science, 161:* 751 – 756, 1968.

Schwartz, G. E., and Weiss, S. M. *Proceedings of the Yale Conference on Behavioral Medicine.* U.S. Department of Health, Education and Welfare, Public Health Service, National Institutes of Health, 1977.

Shapiro, D., Mainardi, J. A., and Surwit, R. S. Biofeedback and self-regulation in essential hypertension. In G. E. Schwartz and J. Beatty (eds.), *Biofeedback: Theory and research.* New York: Academic Press, 1977.

Skinner, B. F. *Science and human behavior.* New York: Macmillan, 1953.

Skinner, B. F. *Beyond freedom and dignity.* New York: Knopf, 1971.

Sloane, R. B., et al. *Psychotherapy versus behavior therapy.* Cambridge, Mass.: Harvard University Press, 1975.

Sloane, R. B., et al. Patients' attitudes toward behavior therapy and psychotherapy. *American Journal of Psychiatry, 133:* 134 – 137, 1977.

Smith, M. L., and Glass, G. V. Meta-analysis of psychotherapy outcome studies. *American Psychologist, 32:* 752—760, 1977.

Somers, A. R. Accountability, public policy, and psychiatry. *American Journal of Psychiatry, 134:* 959 – 965, 1977.

Stolz, S. B., et al. *Report of the American Psychological Association Commission on Behavior Modification.* Washington, D.C.: American Psychological Association, 1977.

Stuart, R. B. Behavioral control of overeating. *Behavior Research and Therapy*, 5: 357 – 365, 1967.

Ullmann, L. P., and Krasner, L. *A psychological approach to abnormal behavior.* Englewood Cliffs, N.J.: Prentice-Hall, 1969.

Wilson, G. T., and Evans, I. L. M. The therapist-client relationship in behavior therapy. In R. S. Gurman and A. M. Razin (eds.), *The therapist's contribution to effective psychotherapy: An empirical approach.* New York: Pergamon Press, 1978.

Wolpe, J. *Psychotherapy by reciprocal inhibition.* Stanford, Calif.: Stanford University Press, 1958.

Wolpe, J. Behavior therapy and its malcontents II: Multimodal eclecticism, cognitive exclusivism, and "exposure" empiricism. *Journal of Behavior Therapy and Experimental Psychiatry*, 7: 109 – 116, 1976.

Index

Index

Addictive behavior, 35 – 36,
  150
Adult offenders, 43
Aged, 43 – 44
Analogue studies, 73,
  103 – 104
  generalizing from, 74 – 78
  relevance of, 74, 78
Anorexia nervosa, 120 – 121
Applied behavior analysis, 6,
  7 – 8
Assessment. *See*
  Measurement
Aversion therapy, 34 – 35

Behavior therapy, 5, 15, 148
  applicability of, 31, 52 – 53,
    152
  clinical practice, 2, 19 – 21
  common questions about,
    22 – 27
  concepts and charac-
    teristics of, 15 – 17,
    149, 151 – 152
  contributions of, 18
  efficacy of, 28 – 46, 30 – 53

history of, 3 – 6
research activity in, 2, 17,
  150
Behavioral medicine, 41,
  140 – 141, 145
Biofeedback, 41 – 42
Box-score strategy, 64,
  152 – 153
  problems with, 65 – 66

Child disorders, 38 – 40, 151
Cognitive behavior
  modification, 6, 13 – 15,
  23
Comparative outcome
  research, 47, 48, 50,
  90 – 91, 95 – 96, 105,
  143, 152
  conceptual and
    methodological problems
    in, 53 – 63
  conclusions from, 51,
    55 – 56, 64 – 66, 152
  priority of, 95 – 96
  results of, 51 – 53
Control groups, 96

Control groups (*continued*)
    nonspecific treatment,
        98 – 100
    no-treatment and
        waiting-list, 97 – 98
Criteria for evaluating
    therapy, 67 – 71, 81, 153.
    See also Box-score
    strategy

Delinquency, 39

Educational applications,
    44 – 45
Ethics, 25 – 27

Flooding, 9, 29, 31 – 32, 55, 66,
    75, 91, 112
Follow-up evaluation, 19, 63,
    69, 71 – 73, 144. *See also*
    Maintenance of behavior

Hyperactivity, 38 – 39

Maintenance of behavior, 33,
    114 – 119, 129 – 131, 145,
    155. *See also* Follow-up
    evaluation
    techniques for, 130
Marital discord, 34 – 35, 150
Measurement, 16, 18,
    126 – 127. *See also*
    Criteria for evaluating
    therapy
    behavioral, 16, 20 – 21,
        59 – 60, 80, 109, 143
    global ratings, 57 – 58, 153,
        157
    multiple methods of, 61, 153
    problems of, 57 – 63
    specificity of, 16, 47, 59, 155
    and therapy outcomes,
        57 – 63, 67 – 73
    traditional methods of, 47,
        68
Mental retardation, 40 – 41

Meta-analysis, 64, 152 – 153
    problems with, 65 – 66
Modeling, 11, 29 – 32, 88 – 89,
    112
    with guided participation,
        30 – 31, 55
    symbolic, 31

Neobehavioristic mediational
    S-R model, 6, 8 – 10
Neurotic disorders, 29
    anxiety and phobic
        reactions, 31, 91,
        107 – 113
    obsessive-compulsive
        disorders, 31, 34, 66
Nonspecific treatment factors,
    25, 98 – 100, 128

Obesity, 117 – 120
Outcome research, 47 – 50,
    53 – 57, 63 – 66. *See also*
    Comparative outcome
    research; Treatment
    evaluation strategies
    assessment in, 57 – 63
    assumptions of, 57
    conventional approach to,
        47 – 66, 143, 152 – 153
    progression of, 95 – 96,
        100 – 103, 105 – 123,
        143 – 144, 154
    recommendations for,
        101 – 104, 124, 142 – 144

Paraprofessional therapists,
    21, 39, 132 – 133, 156
Pharmacotherapy, 39
Psychotic disorders, 36 – 38,
    39 – 40, 151

Quasi-disease model of
    behavior, 5, 15, 61 – 62,
    125, 149

Reinforcement techniques, 8,
29 – 30, 36 – 38, 40,
43 – 44, 111, 120, 130

Self-control techniques, 34,
130
Service delivery, 124,
131 – 136, 156
Sexual dysfunction and
deviance, 121 – 122, 150
Single-case experimental
methodology, 33, 78,
101 – 103, 111, 127, 154
characteristics, 79 – 81
limitations, 81 – 83
Social and community
extensions of behavior
modification, 45
Social learning theory, 6,
10 – 13, 23
reciprocal determinism, 11
self-control, 12
self-efficacy, 12 – 13, 113
Spontaneous remission, 97
Symptom substitution, 16, 23
Systematic desensitization, 9,
18, 29 – 30, 32, 55 – 56, 66,
75, 87, 91, 107 – 111

Therapist-client relationship,
24 – 25, 127 – 129, 136,
146, 149, 155
Therapy research, 47 – 66,
142 – 145. *See also*
Outcome research;
Treatment evaluation
strategies
progression of, 105 – 123
Training, 136, 156 – 157
in clinical psychology,
137 – 138
in psychiatry and medicine,
138 – 140

recommendation for,
141 – 142
Treatment evaluation
strategies, 84, 95 – 96,
99 – 100, 110, 154
client-therapist variation,
92 – 93
comparative, 90 – 91
constructive, 87 – 89
dismantling, 86 – 87
internal structure, 93 – 94
parametric, 89 – 90
problem versus treatment
oriented, 85 – 86
treatment package, 84 – 86
Treatment packages, 84 – 85,
87, 94
Treatment techniques, 19
aversion therapy, 34 – 35
biofeedback, 41, 42
cognitive restructuring,
13 – 14
covert conditioning, 9, 34
flooding, 9, 29, 31 – 32, 55,
66, 75, 91, 112
modeling, 11, 29 – 32, 55,
88 – 89, 112
rational-emotive therapy, 13
reinforcement techniques,
8, 29 – 30, 36 – 38, 40,
43 – 44, 111, 120, 130
sex therapy, 55, 121
systematic desensitization,
9, 18, 29 – 30, 32, 55 – 56,
66, 75, 87, 91, 107 – 111
verbal psychotherapy, 4,
48 – 53, 108 – 109, 123

Verbal psychotherapy, 4,
108 – 109, 123
characteristics of research
in, 53
versus behavior therapy, 4,
48 – 53